Ramblings of an Old Man
Lessons from Life

Bill Entrekin

PUBLISHING
& associates

Copyright

RAMBLINGS OF AN OLD MAN…lessons for life.
Copyright © 2023 Bill Entrekin

Published by Bush Publishing & Associates, LLC
books may be ordered everywhere books are sold and Amazon.com
For further information, please contact:
Bush Publishing & Associates
Tulsa, Oklahoma
info@bushpublishing.com
www.bushpublishing.com

ISBN: 978-1-944566-52-4 (paperback)
ISBN: 978-1-944566-53-1(eBook)

All rights reserved. No portion of this book may be used or reproduced by any means: graphic, electronic or mechanical, including photocopying, recording, taping, or by any information storage retrieval system, without the written permission of the publisher, except in the case of brief quotations embodied in critical articles and reviews.

Printed in the United States of America.

bush
PUBLISHING
& associates

Dedication

This book is dedicated to Liz, a new, wonderful friend and fantastic neighbor who saw something in my writing that I was not able to see myself. She pushed me in a direction I had never even considered, and took the first step for me. Without her, this book would, most certainly, not exist. I am thankful for her encouragement, not only in this effort but in my daily life as well, and, even more so, for her friendship.

Introduction

All of us spend a large portion of our lives attempting to define <u>who we are</u> – to "find ourselves," if you will. Some do so with deliberation, consciously choosing priorities, ideals, and commitments. Others choose a passive approach, changing and choosing as life turns each corner. Some use wealth as a basis for measurement. Others find dimension against a spiritual yardstick; still others use fame, position, title, or status. Most yardsticks, oddly enough, measure only the superficial aspects of our lives and have very little to do with who we truly are. Who we are is a matter of our relationships with others and with God, and how we react to circumstances that confront us. It involves the most basic principles of honesty – with ourselves, as much as with others – our character. It's a worn-out word whose definition has been twisted by a society lacking a yardstick of its own; a society that holds political correctness in higher regard than human life, one where politics is protected at the expense of unborn children, and a society that encourages its members to trade self-esteem, personal effort, and hard work, for a handout. Wealth and poverty are next-door neighbors who have no regard for one another. Performing simple, daily, "acts of random kindness" has become a catchphrase for a passing fad, instead of a true lifestyle. We fail to put into perspective just how much it really matters how much "stuff" we actually have, what vehicle we drive, where we work, where we live, or our income level, all the while lacking the "character" to justify breathing in.

Those moments that truly <u>define</u> our lives are, more often than not, the small details that invade our everyday routines. Oftentimes they go without notice as they rest in our memories, coming to life only as they influence our next decision or the next person in our path. They build, one upon the other, reinforced by repetition, forming governing forces that dictate who we become. They are recognized only through a rear-view mirror, looking back over our lives as time passes. Mistakes carry equal significance with successes in our definition. Failures provide wisdom, determination, patience, and strength. Success offers confidence, opportunity, and momentum, and carries with it responsibility. But the key elements in all of it are the <u>people</u> in our lives. They share with us, they draw from us, and they form the reason for the way we live our lives. Some are woven closely within the daily fabric of our lives while others offer only a glancing blow as they cross our paths. But, make no mistake, all are worthy of our attention. Some require it. Some avoid it. All have an effect on us.

This story was written over the course of more than 20 years and jumps from one decade to another as my memory rambled back and forth from childhood to the present day. It is written in tribute to those people who have taught me, to those who have encouraged me, to those who have cared for me, and to those who have brought me to my knees. It is those people who have collectively shaped the definition of who I am. It is offered to those who follow, as a narrow window into the person that I have come to be and why. It is also a reminder to them to carefully choose the material that constructs the framework of their lives, and the lives of their children.

one

Now is the time for all good men to come to the aid of their country. Now is the time for . . . man, what a stupid phrase to use for typing practice. Whoever came up with that? At least that "quick brown fox . . . jumping over . . . something or other," thing, has all the letters of the alphabet in it – or does it? Anyway, typing is the easy part, especially when you have a computer to check your spelling and grammar for you. Not like it was when I was coming along, no siree! A manual Underwood typewriter was how I learned. Tough times, back then. It can't be that hard to write a book – at least a short one. It doesn't have to be an encyclopedia for goodness' sake. Nobody likes to read that much anyway. Don't have the time anymore. I have always wanted to write a book, but what, exactly, should I write about? Usually, I have plenty to say, but now, nothing comes to mind. Maybe I've got that writer's block – yeah, that's it, writer's block. No, can't be it. I haven't written anything yet. I know! I'll share all my years of experience in . . . uh. . . as a . . . uh . . . all the things I . . . uh. Maybe a novel would be easier – just makeup stuff as you go – doesn't have to be real.

Oh, this is hopeless! Whatever made me think I could write a book anyway? So, what if I made straight "A's" through school – most of it – well a few "B's", and that one "C" in History class – but this ain't History class! Excuse me, *isn't* History class. Mrs. Stokes would be so in my face about a slip like that.

Mary Beth Stokes – my eighth-grade English teacher. It has been a long time since she crossed my mind. She was the *doting old aunt* type that every family seems to have – disconnected a little but somehow obligated to involve herself in your life anyway. Little wonder that she should cross my mind though; she and so many others from my high school years, now decades past. Their skills in English, Geometry, History, Science, and sports now take second place in memory of the concern they had for who I was to become. Considered, then, to be nothing more than meddlesome, they now appear a nearly lost breed whose dedication to their trade extended far beyond their appointed subject matter, and deep into molding the character of those lives entrusted to their care. It sounds quite cliché, but the real curriculum was things like honesty, integrity, and loyalty. They tried to teach us *how* to learn, as well as *what* while pressing us to set goals for ourselves – *and imposing expectations of their own when we did not.* They chose my friends. They formed a team with my parents. They made themselves available to me. If all those teachers could look at me now, I wonder if they would consider their efforts worthwhile. It is truly a shame that depth perception is not as clear facing forward as it is looking back. I now realize just how much I owe all of them. Maybe it isn't so much wisdom that comes with age, as perspective.

But enough of "memory lane". Where was I? Now just settle down. You can do this. Get comfortable. Maybe it's this chair. It is anything *but* comfortable, and it's just too quiet in this house. This house is so big since we "added on" – downright huge – especially when you are here, in the house alone. The only sound I hear is the ice machine gurgling and dropping another cube or two. Oh, and of course, my wind chimes. My daughter, Wendy, gave me those for Christmas last year. I hung them on the back porch just outside my office window. They are perfectly tuned. But then, what else would you expect from a professional musician? Maybe that is why it seems so quiet around here. While the kids were still at home, there was always music in the house – piano, oboe, trumpet, drums, saxophone – something making noise all the time. Yeah, noise! Children are not born knowing how to play those things, you know, and some of them take years, trust me, <u>years</u> to get the hang of. But Wendy stuck with it. Funny, I don't really remember the noisy learning process, so much as the recitals, the performances, the trophies, and the diplomas. Memories also include the football games, the friends at our house, the payments on yet *another* instrument – bigger and better than the last – and one really long band trip to Texas in the dead of winter. And I remember the *fear!* That's right, larger-than-life fear. Wendy was a really good musician. That wasn't just her father's "my-kids-can-do-anything," *slightly* biased opinion. She was really good. Everyone knew it, not just me. How would I ever be able to provide enough challenge to keep her interested in her music – to keep her from being bored? How could I make <u>sure</u> that she would have the opportunity to reach the full potential that I knew she had inside? She had left me in the dust long ago, along with three oboe instructors – one, a performer with the Atlanta Symphony Orchestra – as well as most of her high school class, and the entire band. I was just trying to keep her in sight at this point. There was no hope of keeping up and no use trying.

There had not been money for private schools. Even if there had been, there was a reality in the public school system that, on one hand, I hated for her to face, yet dared not have her miss. We had moved to Fayette County in the first place because of the better school system, but was that enough? Could I have done more? To make matters worse, Kevin was right behind her with every bit of the talent, and every bit the drive, and every bit the potential . . . with a touch of my attitude thrown in to boot. That just doubled my fears. I felt as if their entire futures depended on how well I handled this chapter of this parenting thing, and how well I provided for them at this moment. I had one shot at doing something I knew nothing about and getting it right. I could at least encourage them along the way. I owed them that. I never stopped telling them that they could do anything; there was nothing out of their reach. Their efforts showed that they believed me. All the while, college tuition was clearly out of reach.

I found myself praying often, for some way to get Wendy through college. There had been a savings plan, at one time, but poor business choices on my part had wiped that out. Scholarships were a possibility, but nothing to count on. Then, one Wednesday night, came a true answer to prayer – straight from God, or so it appeared. Actually, it came from Athens, Georgia. The phone call came from the University of Georgia. Wendy had made quite a name for herself at UGA through competitions, summer camps, and clinics there, and had gotten to know the oboe professor very well. It was his voice that offered me the sugar-coated, "I'm-gonna-sell-you-something" greeting. He wasn't selling though, quite the opposite. He asked if Wendy had decided on which college to attend. She had been accepted to both The University of Georgia and Florida State. I told him that we were still considering what each school had to offer, but the final decision, ultimately Wendy's decision, had not been made. He insisted that the University simply "had to have her." He then followed with words that I will never forget: "Just let me know what to write the check for." My answer to prayer had just come right out of his mouth! A free ride and it even included a master's degree! No out-of-state fees, no books to buy, no housing to pay for – and no tuition! I stayed cool, I think, and thanked him for a generous gesture and told him we would get back to him with an answer. Boy, would we get back to him! Hallelujah!!! Wait until I tell Wendy! It's totally her decision of course, but FREE! I am sure that FSU is a good school, but UGA is FREE!!! <u>She</u> must be the one to decide; after all, it is her education and her career on the line, but UGA . . . well, you know... free and all.

I remained true to my word. I left the final decision entirely up to Wendy. We visited both schools, and she weighed all the pros and cons. Finally, she made her decision – the right decision.

The ride home from Tallahassee was utterly miserable. We had left Wendy, preparing to begin her first semester at FSU, starting in just three days. I missed her more with every mile I put between us. Often, I could hardly see the road ahead through the tears. Once back home, it took months to get used to her being away, and years to adjust to being without her. I do not know, to this day, where the money came from. Wendy's grades were more than adequate to earn her a grant for the out-of-state fees, and a part-time job in the music department provided little – very little – spending money. We got student loans for the tuition, and my failing construction business managed to provide the rest . . . somehow. I do not believe in luck, or fate, only divine providence. God picked up the slack. I had done all I could – my very best, I think – knowing all along it was not enough, but it was. Somehow, it just was.

a side note . . .

I carry a single, small, smooth stone in my pocket, everywhere I go. I have carried it for several years now. I have lost it a few times, but it managed to always turn up again. I am convinced that one day, I will lose it for good. But that will actually be alright. It has no monetary value, no sentiment – it is just a rock. I picked it up at some dinner that was sponsored by our church; it was part of a centerpiece on each table and used as an illustration by the pastor. We were each encouraged to take one as a reminder of something – I can no longer remember just what. I do remember that the story was that of the conflict between David and Goliath. It was a natural illustration of the account of David's victory. But since the evening that I picked it up, this one little stone <u>has</u> served as a reminder to me. I have given a lot of thought to the story of David's conquest and have come to recall a few sermons over the years by various pastors, accounting for the details of that day. The story, on the surface, was one of incredible bravery by a very young boy who chose to face a giant far more powerful than he, when no one else would, with nothing more than a slingshot and a rock. One very influential pastor during my youth accounted for David's success against his formidable foe by insisting that it was the very hand of God that guided the stone as it left David's sling, planting it squarely between the eyes of Goliath, killing the longstanding threat, thus ending his reign of terror. It was truly a believable explanation for a very unlikely outcome by this small boy. Further, it gave the ever-present power of God all the credit for the day. I bought into the story. But now, years later, I have come to realize that the pastor's theory was entirely wrong. It was not God who killed Goliath that day – it was David – with a rock and a slingshot, under his own power, by virtue of his own skill.

Now don't misunderstand; I am fully aware of the power of God, and not only believe in His presence that day but His involvement as well. He does get the credit, also, but not from the pastor's perspective. You see, God had long before orchestrated the events of the day, not to mention all of those that led up to it. He had planned the entire event since the day David was born. He had, for instance, put David in the position of a shepherd, before anyone had ever heard of Goliath, let alone David. The job had taught him independence, assertiveness, and quite simply, how to use a sling and a rock – a skill that one would hardly expect to be useful in military warfare. I am sure that in the course of his daily work of protecting his sheep, David had become proficient with a bow and arrow, or maybe a spear or other weapon. But the sling had become his first choice and the one he practiced most often – and became the most comfortable with. Even as good as he was, David must have known that his success was not a given. He must have been afraid. I am sure that over the years David had missed his intended target more often than he might like to admit. The reminder of those missed shots – some, possibly, at critical moments – prompted David to pick up five stones, not just one, as he prepared to meet his adversary. It was David's acquired skill and strength that killed Goliath that day. It was God's unlikely preparation over the years prior that allowed him the opportunity. David's bravery came, not in standing toe to toe with a building-sized threat to his life, but rather in his choice to simply match the abilities God had allowed him to master with the circumstance facing him. He was no match in size or strength, nor did he have an army to back him up. Things could go very wrong, but he had one, single, ability, small though it may be, and was willing to use it for whatever he could accomplish with it. It was all that God required, and that made it enough to fulfill what God wanted done. The stone in my pocket reminds me daily to do what it is that I do, to the best of my ability, and then remain open to God's plan for how my ability is to be used. He does have a plan for my life – it is my job to be obedient. Most of all, it reminds me to look *for the opportunities He places in my path and have the courage to apply my small abilities to whatever circumstances I find myself facing. God will pick up the rest of the slack.*

I guess God has picked up a lot of slack in my life over the years. Funny, I tried never to set lofty goals for my kids. I encouraged them to set goals for themselves and only asked, no, *required* that they do their best at whatever they attempted. When they had done that, I was glad to help with the rest – homework, chores, money. It always made me feel needed. I do not recall a time in my life when God ever set an impossible task before me and demanded that I succeed without help – even this parenting thing. He has only asked that I try my best. Is it possible that God somehow enjoys helping me, as much as I enjoy helping *my* children? I wonder, too, if He ever just needs to feel needed.

two

Maybe I should try to write a book about raising kids. No, maybe just about kids – the stuff they do and what they get into. Nah! Anyone with kids goes through the same things; I can't tell them anything new. And if those people without kids actually believed me, they would probably never have any. It's really not so bad. My kids were great. They still _are_ great. Listening to other parents talk about the problems they had, I kept wondering why I got off so easy. They were both so focused. Wendy knew exactly what she wanted to do with her life by the fifth grade, stuck with it, and totally achieved her goals. Kevin, too. In fact, Kevin was actually involved in his chosen career at the ripe old age of 12.

We had just changed churches, moving to New Hope Baptist after 36 years in a very small congregation just up the road. New Hope boasted a new sanctuary with a seating capacity of around two thousand, already considering double sessions. All my children's friends seemed to go there, and they both – in fact, all of us – fit in from the first day. We began our journey there, perched in the balcony, in the back, where it was safe. We could get lost in the crowd, and hopefully go unnoticed. No one would find us up there. No one would try to give us a job or rope us onto some committee. The trouble was, to get there, we had to walk past the audio console. The eight-foot-long piece of electronic equipment, with over twelve hundred knobs, buttons, and sliders to turn, push, or otherwise mess with, was like a giant magnet to an eleven-year-old boy. He was hooked at first sight and wanted to watch. Now by this point in our lives, Kevin and I had developed such close ties that we could actually read one another's thoughts – our actions and reactions were almost interchangeable. It was spooky sometimes. So, I knew immediately that his definition of "watch" really translated into "touch." I also knew that it was a short trip in his mind from "touch" to "if I took this thing apart, I bet I could figure out how it works."

    I introduced myself and Kevin to Jeff, the sound engineer, and indicated my son's curiosity. Kevin asked to "watch." Imagine my horror when Jeff pulled a stool alongside his and replied, "Not only can you watch, but you can also help!" Jeff had no clue what a "can of worms" he had just opened. He also had no clue about the gratitude I felt for his interest in my son, or of the influence he was about to have in this young life. Kevin was a quick study. He began by pushing the one and only button assigned to him, exactly when he was told to push it. One year later, at twelve years old, he took over Jeff's job as the church's chief sound engineer. By that time, he had taken that thing apart and figured out how it worked. And put it back together, amazingly – **_and,_** had it working better than ever. It was absolutely amazing for me to watch him.

    I have always been in total awe of what he has attempted and accomplished – mostly self-taught. My conservative nature has always trained me to try things in a controlled environment; learn first, then do – a little at first, then work your way up to the harder stuff. Kevin would rather work without a net. Because of his dive-right-in-the-deep-end approach to everything he tried, I assigned myself the task of making sure he was prepared for the occasional, inevitable, failure. That's what a dad has to do, right?

    It is a fine line to walk between encouraging a child that he can be, or do, anything he sets his mind to - and pushing him to try – while offering caution about the possibility of failure. It is confusing enough for me, let alone a child. The summer just prior to entering high school, Kevin decided that he would like to be on the band's drumline when school started, a very prestigious position for a band member, reserved for those percussion students who were born with a pair of drumsticks in their hands. A couple of problems: one, Kevin had never actually played the drums. A minor problem in his eyes I know, but a problem, nonetheless. Two, a first-year band student, even a good one, was not likely to make the drumline right off the bat. A few years of back-up in the percussion section, then, *maybe*, a chance at the front – a chance at best. That was just the way it worked. The more I explained the chances of his <u>never</u> making the drumline, let alone right out of the chute, the more his mind was made up. It wasn't that I did not have faith in his efforts, it was just the odds, and the process to be followed. He had his eyes set on the reward, while I could see only the reality. Drum lessons over the summer and my continued warnings about his probable band position were the best I had to offer. Try-outs rolled around about the end of the first week in school. I braced myself for the obvious. I began to play out in my mind exactly what I was going to say to my son. As try-outs came to an end, I walked over to the band director and began to explain, almost apologetically, my son's expectations . . . and his summer efforts. He interrupted me after only a couple of words. He could not wait to tell me how excited he was to have Kevin on the drumline! Well of course he made it! How better to make a total idiot of his father? I didn't really hear the rest of the instructor's speech – something about...... "an excellent player... and... natural leader . . . and . . . teaching the other students."

Kevin taught <u>me</u> something that day, too. The risk of failure is well worth the possible reward of success. Sometimes you just have to go for it and hope for the best. From that day to this, I still offer words of caution, at times, but with far less veracity than before. In fact, I have tried to broaden a few conservative decisions in my own life, allowing for a little more "This" from time to time.

I was not the first person who had faced the unquenchable spunk in this determined little up-start. Just a few years earlier, his fifth-grade math teacher met with a little attitude herself. Kevin seemed to resent her authority and everyone else's authority. For that matter, he somehow felt that he should be in charge. Being the clever lady that she was, his teacher saw a golden opportunity to put a stop to this arrogance once and for all, and she jumped at it. As she stood at the blackboard, explaining a rather complicated math problem, she could not help but notice that Kevin was paying little attention to her instruction and was, instead, deep in conversation with a very pretty girl sitting behind him. What better tool than utter embarrassment to drive a point home? "Kevin!" she snapped. "Since you seem to have mastered all there is to know about math already, why don't you come up here to the board and explain this problem to the class?" With only a brief, yet thoughtful consideration of his response, he glanced at the board and replied "Sure, I'd be glad to." Through a silence that would have choked any other spirit into submission, Kevin marched toward the front of the room. At this point, complete uncertainty as to her chosen course of action overtook one otherwise confident math teacher. There remained only a glimmer of hope that he might fail. Kevin arrived shortly with chin up and proceeded to retrieve the chalk directly from the hand of his unsuspecting foe. He then turned to the board and completed the problem his teacher had begun – as he explained it to the class – accurately, and succinctly. He then returned the chalk and walked back through the still-silent classroom to take his seat. Well, so much for teaching **him** a lesson! The class continued without further mention of the incident . . . or interruption of Kevin's private conversation with the girl seated behind him.

During the parent-teacher conference that followed later that week (oh, yes there was a conference), his teacher explained that the egg on her face was proof enough that Kevin was certainly bright enough, even bored with the rate of study. His behavior was not even particularly disruptive, but authority had to be respected. I doubt that an actual spotlight suddenly focused on my face at that moment, but it sure felt like it. The notion hit me like a train that this whole issue of authority was entirely *my* fault.

You see, I owned my own construction business at the time, and Kevin worked with me during the summers. It was my responsibility to answer all the questions, whether I actually knew the answers or not. I had to decide. I was the boss. I was in charge. Everyone answered to my authority – right or wrong. I knew all there was to know – no one else; at least that is how Kevin saw things and that is just what he imitated. Though flattered at his following, I was now acutely aware of the responsibility I shouldered. The solution, now, was as evident as the problem: Kevin needed to see me taking instructions from someone else, and learning from them, with some positive outcome.

Kevin and I shared a passion for guns and shooting. We had often talked about someday going to a range and trying our hand at clay target shooting. Skeet shooting was a sport neither of us had any knowledge of. The next Saturday seemed none-too-soon. Neither of us had ever shot enough to become proficient with a shotgun, and Kevin worried a little on the way that he might hit nothing on his first attempt – a golden opportunity to explain that we both would need some instruction to make this work. As I had hoped, we were offered plenty of instruction and needed it. I led the way by asking questions and taking any advice that was offered. Improvement was duly noted as a result, on both our parts.

I can't qualify that outing as the complete solution to the problem, but it certainly served as a turning point. I watched more closely the example I set, now aware that I was under such microscopic scrutiny. I had learned to be proactive in my influence as well, instead of merely passive, realizing the deliberate changes I could evoke if I chose to do so.

Note to my kids: If you are thinking of trying something like this yourself, know that there is one key element that must not be overlooked – insurance. The plan must work the first time; you are not likely to get a second chance, at least an effective one, so be sure your plan is foolproof before you start. I need to remember to tell Kevin, someday, that I had spent Friday afternoon at the shooting range, as well, prior to our Saturday morning venture. I do not wear "egg" very well.

Hopefully, I was able to teach Kevin a few things as he was coming along. He certainly taught me a great deal. In many ways, I have come to depend on him, as he once depended on me. He was, by this time, teaching Jeff the finer points of audio control at our church. He quickly became quite proficient at the shooting range, as I knew he would. Roles seem to constantly change as I get older. The student becomes the instructor. Children become parents. Parents become grandparents. Grandparents become children again. Those once dependable, become dependent. I sit and watch my own father struggle to read a restaurant menu. I find myself raising my voice to be heard through his pair of hearing aids, already at full volume. I offer a little support to his elbow as he attempts to negotiate a couple of steps and an uneven walkway leading to my front door. Then, as I look into my morning mirror, and consider what must undoubtedly be lies and exaggerations presented to me by my own reflection, I am reminded of my own continued growth toward childhood, once again. It is at least a little comforting to know that there are capable hands waiting to offer support to my elbow, someday.

    Kevin and I no longer spend time together at the shooting range. I miss that. I still try to go as often as I can – but alone now. I never go, however, without the memory of every afternoon we spent together there. Maybe the reason I still go, in part, is in hopes that our paths might cross there once again.

three

Let's see. What do I spend most of my time doing? I could write about that. Working. That's boring. Church – spend a lot of time there. Maybe I'll write about church . . . or God . . . or talking to God . . . or God talking to me. Like that deal with the grandkids. That would probably get me *committed*. Part of the family already thinks I'm about half a bubble out of plumb. The rest think I'm just a lucky guesser. At least I know the real truth. God *does* tell me things from time to time when I bother to listen. Oh, I don't mean I can hear Him out loud or anything, but still . . . it was a Saturday, around noon, when I walked into McDonald's with a Quarter Pounder on my mind. As I approached the counter, I noticed a little blonde-haired girl standing on her tiptoes, struggling to shove a handful of change over the lip of the counter in anticipation of the ice cream cone the cashier was holding. She shifted back onto her heels and waited patiently as the clerk counted out the change. She was too young to even understand what the lady meant when she said "I'm sorry, sweetie, but you're a nickel short. Do you have any more money?" The toddler was confused but remained steadfastly awaiting her dessert. I reached into my pocket and slid the nickel across the counter, prompting the clerk to release the little girl's ice cream from her hostage grip. As I finished placing my order, I heard a female voice over my shoulder say "Thank you. That did not go unnoticed, I assure you." Mom, apparently. The little girl had caught my attention for some reason other than just the need for a little ice cream money. The cone seemed nearly as big as she was as she headed back to her seat, now guided by Mom's hand, paying more attention to licking than walking. The petite little doll had blue eyes and an ear-to-ear smile. I found it hard to take my eyes off her. It finally occurred to me that maybe I had met her for a reason. I began to evaluate the situation a little more closely. Did Mom have anything to eat? She had not offered to return my nickel. Maybe she had no more money. Was this, in fact, desert, or the entirety of her lunch? How were they dressed? Was this just some chance meeting or was there some additional need that I was intended to meet? No, everything seemed in order. Drinks and the remains of two full lunches were still evident on the table. Both were clean and smartly dressed. They left just ahead of me and got into a late-model car, also in good condition. My mind had just created some need that did not exist. The entire incident had been, despite my active imagination, just a chance meeting with a little girl who was five cents short of an ice cream cone. Nothing more.

 Six months later, my daughter would announce that I was going to be Grandpa for the first time. Nobody could ever be as excited as I was. My thoughts alternated between the idea of a new baby in the family and the health and well-being of my daughter. A few anxious moments surrounding her own birth prompted prayers for an easy delivery, without repeat complications. Just under three months later when the announcement came, Wendy and the baby immediately became the single topic of conversation throughout the family. Every "congratulation" came attached to yet another horror story surrounding the birth of every child in the clan. Talk about a really comforting bunch! It was about a month later, driving to a construction site to measure a house for cabinets when it happened. Call it a "vision" if you like, but I think that is a bit strong. My mind just drifted for a bit. The thoughts of the job I was headed to and the schedule for the remainder of the afternoon were suddenly interrupted by the image of a little girl fixed in my mind. She was a toddler, with bright blonde hair and radiant blue eyes. She was holding the hand of my daughter, as they walked along together. I immediately knew the face of the little girl. I had seen her in McDonald's, a few months earlier. I had actually seen my own granddaughter before I even knew she was to be born. Well, almost. The actual smiling face of my own granddaughter was not identical to the little ice cream seeker, but the statistics were all the same. I pulled to the side of the road at the very next place wide enough to get off the pavement, picked up my cell phone, and called my daughter. With the utmost of certainty, I informed her that she was going to have a little girl – with blue eyes – and, as a toddler, at least, blonde hair. Wendy knew that I was not a drinker, so that couldn't be my problem. She gratefully acknowledged the information and proceeded to cautiously question the source of this great revelation. God. It was God who told me. "Oh," she replied, still a little skeptical, no matter how much she wanted to trust.

When I had the opportunity to share this newly revealed information with others in the family, without exception, each one ignored the news before them and proceeded to make their own assessments of probability, based on how Wendy was carrying the baby, the percentage of boys or girls born into which branch of the family, or some other old wife's tale that could not possibly have any bearing on the <u>fact</u> that Wendy was going to have a little girl because **God had told me so!** Sorry, I still get beside myself a little about it all. What do you have to do to convince somebody that this was no *guess*, but rather an absolute confirmation? A sonogram just a few weeks later proved my "guess" to be a <u>lucky</u> one. I gave up.

Now, a few more months into the pregnancy, and the due date absolutely certain to be no later than the first week in April, it happened again; this time, in the middle of the night. I woke up, suddenly, in response to an announcement by a nurse, informing the waiting family that Wendy had just given birth to a baby girl, 6 lbs. 14 oz. The calendar on the wall behind the nurse read the 17th. This time I was way out on a limb. I asked Wendy what she had planned for the 17th of April. She said she would most certainly be home with a new baby by that time, in at least a week or so. Her doctor had confirmed, yet again, that things were moving faster than expected and she should be prepared to go early. Nope. It was going to be the 17th – not a day earlier.

Morgan Abigail was born on April 17th, weighing 6 lbs. 14 oz., with a full head of red hair, just like her mom's. Somehow that red hair made every bit of my *guesswork* inaccurate. By the time Morgan began to walk, however, her beautiful red hair had turned, down to the last hair, to bright blonde. Me and God . . . we knew it all along. I was so certain from the beginning that I wrote a letter to "my granddaughter," telling her all about what had happened, what a special little girl she was, and how I could hardly wait to meet her. I mailed it to myself. It sits in my desk drawer, waiting for the appropriate time to give it to her. Maybe God will tell me when.

At three years old, Morgan marched over to the sofa where I lay watching television and proudly displayed a tee shirt that read "I'm going to be a big sister." Grandchild number two was officially on the way. No roadside revelation this time. No voices in the middle of the night – just an ordinary dream. I was standing in the hospital. The date was March 23rd, though I'm not sure just how I knew that – I was just sure of the date. Someone in a white uniform – nurse, again, I guess – was holding a baby; a really big baby . . .at least 8 pounds, likely more. It was a boy, with a chubby round face, dark brown hair, and blue eyes. Wendy was not totally convinced this time around either, but far less suspicious of this latest news. I couldn't get the weight exactly but was certain we had a linebacker on the way. Time, and yet another sonogram, indicated that the boy that was on the way was indeed a big one.

Wendy was a week beyond her expected due date, but not yet having reached the 23rd. Plans were set in motion to speed things up a bit. Because of his size, and already at full term, Wendy was advised to report to her doctor's office on the 20th to finalize plans to induce labor, probably later that day. The doctor confirmed the need to make things happen, but postponed the blessed event until the next day, as it was already mid-afternoon, and the baby could certainly wait the night. He instructed her to call the hospital in the morning to check their delivery load for a convenient time to come in. She returned home, a little disappointed and a lot uncomfortable to await another day. Everyone must have had the same plans for the 21st because maternity was full for the morning shift. The afternoon looked open, though, so she could come in later at her leisure. Packed and headed out the door, Wendy answered the phone to yet another delay. Babies were everywhere and there was no need to come in just yet if there was no emergency. The 22nd arrived, and finally a breather at the hospital. Through a barrage of I-told-you-so's, I held my ground for the 23rd. So did the baby. He waited all day and most of the night. Kalen Aric was born on March 23rd, with blue eyes, and brown hair, at **9 lbs. 8 oz.** No one made fun of my *guesswork*. They weren't about to acknowledge my accuracy, either. No one said a word – didn't have to. I knew. Me and God knew.

There is one other thing that no one knew but me – not to this day. There was something that kept bugging me about this second grandchild's name. Rob and Wendy had made no mention of what they had intended to name the baby, holding the announcement until our first visit following his arrival. Every time I gave the matter any thought, the letter "K" kept coming to mind. I could never get past the name "Kevin" – that of my own son – but knew for certain it would not be a duplicate. There was not another single family member whose name started with a "K," so I finally gave up. I did, however, take a small piece of paper and print a large "K" in the middle of it, stuck it in my pocket, and carried it to the hospital with me. I could feel it nearly burn a hole in my pocket as Rob introduced **Kalen** Aric.

I can already picture myself taking him to the shooting range with me, just as I did with Kevin years ago. I can hardly wait. I bought him a shotgun, two weeks before he was born.

I guess, at least I hope, all grandparents have some special attachment to their grandchildren – something only they feel between themselves. I certainly do. I have seen them both push through crowds of family to find me – only me, yelling for "Grandpa" all the way. There is a connection between us that I cannot begin to explain. It feels as though we have known one another for far longer than their short lives. Truth is, we <u>have</u> known one another longer. Say what you will, God introduced us.

I was listening during those two events. I heard His voice. I often wonder how many times he might have spoken when I wasn't listening, or just could not hear Him over the noise. Maybe there have been times when the crowd of other voices – business, finances, problems, worries, or self-indulgence, have drowned out the quiet instructions that I needed most. I think, perhaps, a little more "listening" time might be in order. There may well have been other times when I have heard the voice of God but did not recognize it – maybe because I did not want to believe what He had to say. Mislabeled as a hunch, a premonition, a whim, or just an idea that I could not get out of my head, I was hearing His voice without giving Him credit for the conversation. However, he chooses to speak, I am sure He enjoys talking with us as much as He does hearing from us. By the way, Morgan is going to be famous as an adult; maybe as a musician, maybe an actress, an author, a businesswoman…who knows? We'll just have to wait and watch. God told me.

four

Man! I can't believe I fell asleep sitting here at my computer! What time is it anyway? I must get to bed. I have a project due early in the morning, and I wanted to save some time in the afternoon to do a little more work on this house. It seems I always have something torn out. The place is looking pretty good, though, if I do say so myself. I am more than ready to have all the unfinished projects wrapped up. It is hard to believe that we have lived here for over twenty years. Wendy and Kevin did most of their growing up here. What is even harder to believe is that I have lived in five houses, two apartments, and one trailer, and have never ventured further than ten miles from my starting point. I actually lived in one house twice. That was my grandmother's house.

My parents brought me home from the hospital to a newly constructed, three-room cottage. It was designed to be the future detached garage of a home my dad planned. It sat on the lot next door to the home of my mom's parents. Dad had purchased one acre from them and managed to save enough for materials for the small structure. Built it himself. Cozy though it was, it provided for us very well for nearly five years. It was at that time that my grandfather (Mom's Dad) died – of lung cancer. The two-bedroom home next door consisted of about nine hundred square feet of floor space, consisting of a living room, dining room, a small kitchen, single bath, an enclosed back porch, and a screened porch off the living room. There was far more space there than my grandmother ever anticipated living in alone, and an improvement, though slight, of our own current living quarters. We moved in and shared the space with her.

There were certainly countless memories created in that house during my early childhood stay. Sunday meals with the entire family, an old hand-crank, wringer-type washing machine out under a huge oak tree in the backyard, a water well just off the back steps with a bucket to draw water, a sleepy swing hung between a couple of crooked pines, and a garden out back full of every vegetable imaginable, are only a few of the precious memories. One particular memory stands out, painfully, above all the rest.

I dare say that I managed to grow up without getting into nearly the trouble that many children do. But, as an only child, I did find an occasional opportunity to stretch the limits of my imagination and the patience of my mother. She remains, to this day, a very loving woman who would never consider any form of abuse or allow it by anyone else. Still, she had a tolerance level that I tested on a regular basis. My punishment was never swift to come, but always the same when it did. Just outside the door to the screen porch grew a tall bush with long, straight, stems, dark green leaves, and beautiful purple blooms in the Spring. It served a purpose far more familiar, though than mere landscape decoration. Mom, having taken all she could stand of my testing, would break off one of those branches about two feet long, and strip off all the leaves except a couple near the tip end. When those leaves were gone, she could be fairly certain that the back of my legs and the seat of my pants had suffered enough. It would always take quite some time before the stinging reminder of my wrongdoing would subside. Though I had earned every session and even escaped a few more that I deserved, I never did learn to like purple flowers very much.

With only one bedroom to be shared between my mom, my dad,

and myself, it was evident enough that this arrangement would not suffice for long. Dad began work, almost immediately, building the home next door that he had planned from the start. Working on the home just on Saturdays – and doing almost all the work alone – the project was slow to say the least. At six years old, I could hardly wait for Saturday mornings and the opportunity to help with the nailing or sawing, or whatever there was to do that day. I am sure I was much more in the way than I was "help," yet Dad always found a way to involve me in the process that made me feel vital to the cause. To my mother's absolute horror, I even learned to nail on roofing, still only six. Dad would locate each shingle with nails in the outside corners. My job was to hammer the two nails in the middle. We roofed the entire house that way. That began the fascination with construction that I would carry with me for the rest of my life. I still tear up stuff, just for the opportunity to build it back in a different fashion. Another five years passed before we moved from my grandmother's house into the completed, fifteen hundred square foot "dream home" next door, with my own room. It was there I would live until the day I married.

A lot of shuffling around took place over the next few years. My parents rented out the small, "never-became-a-garage" house behind theirs to a variety of families, through a variety of circumstances. Finally, my grandmother actually moved into the smaller home and rented her house to tenants instead. As for Linda and I, we began in two different apartments, and it was time for another move. The space was inadequate, and the neighbors had become intolerable in the apartment project. As our search began, my grandmother's current tenants announced a move of their own. I jumped at the chance and moved back into my grandmother's house which marked the end of apartment leasing.

I backed the truck up to the door and dropped the tailgate, beginning the welcome chore of unpacking the hodge-podge of mismatched furniture and boxes of stuff that we had collected. As I raised the first box off the truck bed, I noticed my hand saw tucked neatly against the wheel well for the move. I knew what I had to do. More importantly, it had to be done now. My mission was clear in my own mind, but my wife had a curious look on her face as she watched me put down the box I was holding, pick up the saw, and round the corner of the house toward the screen porch door. There it stood. Taller and more threatening than ever – my worst childhood nightmare – purple flowers and all. Wondering if I had, in fact, finally gone over the edge, my wife now stood watching as I sawed the flowering source of pain down level with the dirt - all the while explaining to her my motivation for the effort. The rest of the boxes and furniture were indeed a joy to unload, with my front-corner nemesis now laid to rest.

I guess I really cut down that bush out of pure vengeance, as though somehow its demise would repay my experiences of years past. Had I left it, I have no doubt that it would have provided a constant reminder of the very unpleasant memories associated with having lived there, not to mention, a reminder of my own wrongdoing. With it gone, I never gave those times a second thought. What I was cutting out was an association with a bad memory, not a bush. Left to sprout again, even thrive in our lives, we sometimes actually nurture those things that can ultimately steal the spotlight of better times. Things like grudges, harsh words, quarrels, misunderstandings, and even out-and-out battles, are part of every person's life. How much and how long they will affect our lives depends on how much of our lives we allow them to occupy. Usually, it comes down to a conscious choice to hang on to them. Life is all too short (old cliché, still, appropriate) to spend it dredging up old pain. A true sign of maturity is how quickly we are able to forgive, or resolve, or sometimes, just get beyond those memories that would stand between us and our own peace of mind. We seem to prefer dragging around baggage, often empty baggage, just to prove our scars. Scars are not pretty. We all have them, but they are nothing to brag about. Pruning of unwanted branches allows for fuller, healthier growth of more useful plants. I am likely to remember that old swing between the pines in the front yard with much more clarity simply because I don't have to pull back the branches on one particular bush in order to see it.

five

My dad managed to impart a lot more wisdom than just the finer points of roofing installation as I was growing up. He taught me how to do almost anything around the house, of course, but, more than that, he taught me to at least make an attempt at those things I did not know how to do. The failure rate among those who make no effort is 100%. Some lessons involved a few hours of instruction, a little hands-on experience, and then a solo effort. Others, some of the more valuable ones, have taken a lifetime. Sundays were a time for family. Church came first – always – then lunch, often with a crowd of aunts, uncles, and cousins. Mom would cook something akin to Christmas dinner about every other week. Dad was always at her side, supportive, and usually up to his elbows helping with the preparation. Dad was a pretty fair cook himself. Mom was in charge of the kitchen as was evident by the instructions she doled out to the capable, and the reprimands to those under foot. Most of the family took full advantage of the excellent service offered and parked in the living room to catch up on the family gossip. Such was the scene on a particularly memorable Sunday. It had been a long week for Dad – traveling through the week, as usual, calling on customers, trying to stir up a few sales.

To top it off, it was summer, and the garden was in. Dad planted almost a full acre every year, worked it by hand, and managed to produce enough vegetables to feed us through the fall, store enough for the winter, and all the while feeding the rest of the family and half of the community. No matter how tired at the end of the day, he managed to spend a couple of hours in the garden - and all day on Saturday. When the weather offered temperatures that were nothing less than scorching, he would be hard at it by daylight during the week and tend the garden until he had to leave for work.

Sunday may be a "day of rest" by design, but Dad did not feel too rested today. A nap would be a far more welcome way to spend the afternoon than entertaining a mooching family. Still, he managed to scurry around with a smile, guided by Mom's prompting. Lunch over, the table cleared, and the last dish in the sink in Mom's care, Dad decided to slip into the living room with the others and join those complaining of having eaten too much, as usual. To his surprise and delight, though the room was lined with stuffed relatives, his favorite recliner sat empty. He strolled over, satisfied that his kitchen duty was complete. With his back toward the chair, steadying himself with one hand on each arm of the chair, his knees unlocked, and he headed toward the long-awaited comfort beneath him. Such was not to be. Somewhere around halfway between vertical and comfortable, Mom's voice rang out from the kitchen. "Cecil!" The response was virtually automatic and mechanical. Whatever muscular mechanism that had been set in motion to place him in that chair shifted into reverse, and up he rose. He never touched the seat of that recliner. A thin smile crossed his lips as he returned to the kitchen for further instruction. There were a couple of smiles around the room, as well, from those not too self-absorbed to witness the event and to have heard Mom's beckoning. The general opinion was the same among the aunts and uncles present: "Pauline never lets up on him," or "She works him too hard, all the time," or "She never lets him get a minute's peace." All of them were oblivious, of course, to the fact that all his efforts today had been put toward <u>their</u> benefit, with a minimum of assistance or gratitude. Worst of all, they all defined Dad as "hen-pecked." Admittedly, I even interpreted the thin smile I had spotted as a hint of embarrassment as he responded to Mom's slightest whim.

Something about this picture, though, contradicted itself. My father was far from the weak link in this family. Mom and Dad discussed every decision and made them together, but it was always Dad who controlled the final vote – and that with Mom's willing submission. They never argued – <u>never!</u> Mom never questioned Dad's motives or direction, and he never gave her cause. They formed a unified front for me, interchangeable when it came to reward or discipline. They acted, in every way, as one person, with Dad taking the leading role for the duo. No, this was no hen-pecked husband before us today. This was not a man dominated by an overbearing wife, nor a wife who wished to be. So, what was it? What force could drive anyone to be so responsive to another's wishes? For some reason, it seemed, he just wanted it that way.

I have given thought, at times, to what he must have set aside for her. No regrets, you understand, and certainly no resentment of Mom, but surely there must have been goals or dreams that he discarded on her behalf. That did not make life any less on any level – for him, or for the both of them. Just different. I am convinced that Dad lived exactly the life he wanted and would never change a single moment. But I also believe that he could have achieved just about anything he set his mind to. I can't help but wonder – what if……….? Dad never wondered, or, at least, it never showed.

It would not be until August 4th, 1972, reinforced by all the years that have followed since, that I would truly grasp what it was that provided such motivation in my dad. At 7:30 on that evening, Linda Ann White and I were married. The behavior I had witnessed so often growing up did not seem so strange to me at all anymore. Never had I known someone that I was perfectly prepared to kill for, or perfectly willing to die for. That person was, and remains, Linda. I have come to realize that the smile on Dad's face that Sunday was not an embarrassment, but rather a deep-rooted joy in being able to please my mom. Nothing in his life meant more than making her happy, keeping her safe, or protecting her peace of mind. They have, to this day, an unspoken understanding of one another that only years of effort can produce. And, still, nothing makes <u>Dad</u> happier than some small opportunity to please his mate, by conscious choice, not obligation.

    I share his spirit. I share his source of joy. Call it genetics if you like. Consider it, even, my upbringing – mimicking the daily example set by my father. I prefer knowing that the true source is Linda – who she is, how she cares for me, and who we are together. I can only hope to achieve the level of expertise that Dad has reached at making a marriage look like a walk in the park - effortless in appearance; indestructible; permanent; the focus of his very existence. Nothing ever seemed to shake him. If it did, it never showed. Job could have taken lessons in patience from my father. I still need a little practice with that half-way-to-the-chair maneuver, though, and a little more of his patience as well. Just when I think maybe I am beginning to get a handle on how it should be done, I glance over at Dad and realize I need a <u>lot</u> more practice.

six

It was surprising, in a way, that Mom and Dad ever got married at all. He was much too "rough" for Mom's liking, and she refused to date him while they were in school. Following graduation, World War II was in full swing, and Dad decided to enlist in the Navy. It wasn't called the Navy then. Since there was no actual Air Force at the time, the combined unit was known as the Naval Air Corps. The process for enrolling was a little diffcrent then. Recruitment stations were few and far between and the nearest one to Dad's home in Fairburn was in Americus, Georgia, just southwest of Columbus. It was about two weeks before Christmas and Dad chose a Sunday afternoon to make the drive down and get the ball rolling. He borrowed his brother's car – a DeSoto, I believe – and solicited the company of his girlfriend at the time (not my mom) to go with him. Upon arrival, he began the process of filling out all the required paperwork – medical records, etc. Then there was the physical, a review by the recruitment board, and finally, if all went well, acceptance. Everything was done on the same day to recruit new men as quickly and as efficiently as possible, to keep the war effort fully staffed. Dad had made it perfectly clear that he intended to enlist immediately but report to duty just after Christmas, allowing time to spend the holidays with family before heading off. Everyone seemed to understand and be perfectly receptive to the idea. Everything went smoothly up until the weigh-in. There was a minimum weight requirement of 110 lbs. to join the Corp. Dad was shy of that minimum by a couple of pounds. He returned to the waiting area, where he managed to find a glass and a water fountain. He began drinking water – as much as he could hold. After about an hour, he returned to the medic in charge and asked to be re-weighed. Dad weighed in at 110 lbs. exactly.

Now back in the holding area, Dad and his friend awaited a ruling, and instructions for his date to report. A gruff-looking Sargent soon emerged and called his name along with 25 or 30 others. "You are all on the next bus out" he barked. "You don't understand," Dad explained. "I'm not supposed to go in until after the holidays." The grin on the sergeant's face suggested otherwise as he replied, "You signed the papers young man – you belong to Uncle Sam now." Dad's girlfriend took the keys to the car, faced with the task of driving it back alone, returning it to my uncle, and telling Dad's Mom and the rest of the family that he was gone – to Pennsylvania – without so much as a goodbye. What is more, Dad (as did everyone else who joined) had enlisted "for the duration" of the war. That meant he was in until the war was over, no matter how long it took. Dad spent Christmas Day scrubbing the pine floors on a barracks in Pennsylvania.

Following boot camp, Dad found himself stationed in Pensacola, Florida, along with his brother Herbert who had enlisted just after Dad. The base there was assigned the task of training pilots for overseas duty. The training was fast-paced, frantic, and anything but thorough. If you could get a plane off the ground and back down again, mostly in one piece, you were a pilot, and off to war. Dad's task as chief flight mechanic was to keep those planes in working order, patch them up as needed when they crashed or were shot full of holes, and get them back on the front line. It also fell his duty, now and then, to retrieve the pieces of those planes from the local swamp, lost thereby green pilot-wanna-be's, and sometimes, even the pieces of those pilots themselves. Friends of his at times.

Pensacola proved to be a walk in the park compared to those assigned overseas. Orders could change any day, and one day they did. Dad was being assigned to overseas duty, right in the middle of the action, along with several others serving alongside in Florida. The day came and he packed his gear, loaded up, and was transported to a waiting transport plane. As the door to the plane closed, a hand reached through and opened it back. Dad was singled out and instructed to return to the base. Back in familiar surroundings, he reported to his commanding officer to find out just what the problem was. His C.O. explained "I am required to maintain a specific, minimum staff to operate this base. That includes at least one person with a first-class ranking. You are the last first class on the base, so you have to stay."

There was obviously a lot of pressure on everyone in the country around that time, none of whom felt it more than those in the military. They all managed to look for some means to blow off a little steam from time to time. The pressure just added a more dramatic twist to things. Now there was a dirigible hangar on the Pensacola base. We now know them more commonly as blimps. This type of aircraft was in service in the military for years, including throughout the course of World War II. As you can imagine, the hanger had an enormous ceiling height to allow a proper fit, with huge sliding doors on each side, opposite one another. One particularly cocky new pilot bragged that he could fly in one side of the hanger and out the other without touching a thing. His attempt was impressive, and successful, but not unnoticed by his authorities. His antics got him court-martialed immediately. Yet another pair of thrill-seekers, seeking to have a little "fun" with their officer in charge, decided to dangle him by his ankles from the third-story barracks balcony. Fun for them, at least – that is until they let him slip and dropped him to his death. Court-martialed as well, but with far more serious consequences this time. Nothing seemed off limits in an effort to maintain one's own sanity. Some just went too far.

seven

By now, Dad had somehow convinced Pauline Harper to talk with him, write to him, and even go out on a date whenever he managed to get back home. Getting back home usually occurred via a Harley Davidson "Hog" that Dad had acquired – the largest model of motorcycle that Harley Davidson made at the time. The Naval base had a chrome plating machine, intended for use on Navy equipment, but well suited for plating every part on the bike engine, one by one. No one noticed that Dad had removed parts from the engine and carried them into the shop with him day after day, one at the time, and returned them to the bike in a much brighter condition. It did not take long and the "Hog" was a shiny work of art. He often rode double back to Fairburn along with his brother, Herbert. Herbert was dating my aunt-to-be, Rilla, and Dad was now seeing my eventual mom, Pauline.

On one such trip, Herbert was driving with Dad on the back. They usually pushed their speed to whatever the road conditions would allow to be able to spend as much time at home as possible. About halfway home they rounded a blind curve to encounter a full-grown mule standing in the center of their lane. Uncle Herbert swerved as far to the right as he could to avoid disaster. At the last second, the startled mule lunged forward and total calamity was avoided, but only by inches. The mule's coarse tail actually brushed across Herbert's knuckles, leaving bleeding cut marks stretching the width of his hand.

They employed the bike regularly for the home-bound trips, as well as local use around Pensacola on a daily basis. It had rained one Saturday night and left the tarmac on the base standing in water. Dad was headed across the base, this time wearing his dress whites, including his bell-bottom pants – his own doing. (The Navy approved, and Dad's upholstery experience taught him use of a sewing machine that most did not have, so he picked up a little spending money "belling" the bottom of the other sailors' pants, $2.00 per pair). The base was crisscrossed by railroad tracks. To ensure that his white pants stayed clean, Dad put his feet up on the handlebars of the bike. He crossed one of those sets of tracks at an angle and the bike slipped out from under him, ruining a full set of dress whites, not to mention quite a bit of much-needed skin around his knees, elbows, and shoulders. He managed to get up and walked to the nearest phone where he called a fellow sailor who had been trying to buy the bike from Dad for several months. He informed the friend that the bike was for sale, provided he picked it up from the middle of the tracks where it remained. He let the bike go for $300.00.

Lieutenant Mayer was Dad's commanding officer. He, too, had a similar feminine interest north of Pensacola – Atlanta, to be exact, just about 20 miles north of Fairburn. Rank would afford him the opportunity to check out an airplane for "training" purposes. He needed a co-pilot or a navigator on such missions and Dad fit that bill quite nicely. Dad was never a pilot, nor a qualified co-pilot, but who was checking credentials anyway? They would fly to Atlanta where each would be picked up by respective waiting parties, then returned to the airport in time to make it back at the end of their leave. Lt. Mayer had one, minor, bothersome habit – he liked to drink while on leave – a lot! The routine was always the same. His girlfriend would return him to the plane, drunk beyond belief, and Dad would pile him into the pilot's seat. The Lieutenant somehow managed to stay awake just long enough to get the plane off the ground, then pass out for the remainder of the flight, leaving Dad to fly them back to Pensacola. He followed beacons along the way, placed for that particular purpose, or he traveled along major roadways. Nearing the base, Dad would rouse Mayer to once again take the controls and land the plane.

One morning Dad was confronted by Lt. Mayer, along with two other officers, and sternly ordered to load an awaiting plane with guns and ammunition, now in a large heap, just outside the plane on the ground. "You're coming with us," Mayer barked. "We have an assignment to carry out." It was the middle of a war. Guns, ammunition, and "assignment" could not be a very inviting combination, but, these were orders. Dad loaded the plane, then took his place inside, as they taxied down the runway and lifted off. Totally out of his mind by now, Dad asked the nature of this exact mission. Lt. Mayer, as straight-faced as he could muster, replied "We have been told that the <u>pheasants</u> are taking over Arizona and they have to be stopped." The four of them spent a leisurely day pheasant hunting, somewhere in Arizona, and returned to base that evening.

One of Dad's least favorite duties fell in rotation with all the other sailors on base. On a small island, just off the coast of Pensacola, there was a makeshift prison camp that housed a dozen or so Japanese prisoners. In 12-hour shifts, the sailors took turns walking guard duty around the perimeter of the fenced-in prison camp. Flown out to the island, with no way back, or any means of communication, you served alone until your relief was brought out for the next shift. It fell to Dad's lot to serve one very cold Winter's day. With his 12 hours almost up, Dad found himself exhausted and cold beyond belief. Some hot coffee and a stiff cot would be a most welcome sight. But his relief was late for some reason, so his shift continued for yet another hour. Then another, then another. His relief did not show at all that night and he spent the bitter cold evening walking a 24-hour guard duty. The closest, he said, that he had ever come to freezing to death.

The saddest part of all this was the prisoners themselves.

Though a guard had to be present at all times, the prisoners would not have left had the gate been standing wide open. The conditions under which they had served were deplorable. No warm clothing or a decent place to sleep, and with little or no food. They worked without time off, around the clock. The U.S. prison camp, though basic to say the least, provided them with a dry place to sleep, warm blankets, and plenty of good food. They were most appreciative of the treatment they received and were not about to give it up.

eight

Gosh, it is really getting hot in here. Where is the thermostat set on that air conditioner, anyway? You can really tell that summer is here. It seems like we skipped Spring altogether and went straight from dead Winter to mid-summer overnight. I need to be headed to the lake in this kind of weather, or a vacation somewhere. Yeah, like I'm actually going to get to take a vacation this year. There is just too much to do. And trips are so expensive! It seems we used to go somewhere every year, that is when I was growing up. Sometimes we would head for the beach, or the mountains. Occasionally we would visit relatives – boring. One year we spent the week in Washington D.C., and another, two full weeks driving through the Western U.S.; St. Louis, Yellowstone, the Grand Canyon, Arizona, Texas, and back home. The best years were those when we took a week and went fishing. The whole family would go . . . Mom, Dad, Grandma, usually an aunt and uncle, and even a cousin or two. For several years in a row, we set out for the same little fish camp in central Florida. The place was run down, even then, but in my eyes, it represented a completely new world, with more to explore than

I could cover in just one short week – far from the all-too-familiar yard at home. This was truly a long-awaited adventure. It took all day to get there, but it was always worth the wait. Four or five little two-room cottages waited at the end of a poorly maintained dirt road. Electricity and running water were decided luxuries in this setting, with air conditioning simply too much to hope for. The overhead canopy of towering oaks and palms were ample substitutes. Compact screen porches on the front of each unit faced the water and invited a cool breeze off the lake each evening after dinner. A single screened door opened onto a set of steps which led to a narrow concrete walk connecting each cottage to the next. The walk trailed down a gentle slope, winding around shrubs and huge trees along the way, and ending at the boat shed and dock. Several flat-bottom, aluminum boats were tied, two to the slip, each outfitted with a small outboard motor, a five-gallon gas tank, and a couple of wooden paddles.

The routine usually followed the same pattern. Midday was much too hot to spend on the open water. Besides, the fish didn't bite very well anyway. That time was reserved for lunches and naps, and exploring every crevice of this fascinating surrounding. Early morning and late afternoon outings were times for serious fishing. I was usually given the option for either a morning or afternoon trip each day, lacking the stamina or the patience to endure both. I am not sure whether the lack of patience was shorter on my end or my parents, at times, but I still got in my share of wetting a hook. When not out in the boat, the water off the end of the dock was literally teeming with fish and offered plenty of entertainment. The adults would alternate the chore of babysitting/food preparation from day to day, always with at least one dinner from the day's catch.

Lake Apopka looked like an ocean to me, as we set out one morning just as the sun was clearing the lake's edge. The mirror-flat water seemed to stretch as far as I could see. The morning air was actually cool, and the only sound was the hum of the little outboard pushing us along in search of a likely-looking spot to anchor. Armed with my Zebco "33" rod and reel, a six-year-old's most prized possession, I was fully confident in a successful catch by day's end. And catch fish we did! Lots of fish. Hundreds of fish. Cooler after cooler, full of fish! Bream, bluegill, shellcracker, channel catfish, bass – by now I could identify every species, and could hold my own when it came to hauling them into the boat. Four of us in a boat, my mom, dad, grandmother, and I had anchored just a few yards offshore and begun casting back toward a blanket of lily pads. It hardly mattered where you dropped your line, a bite was sure to come quickly.

And so, it went on for nearly an hour, when, as suddenly as though someone had flipped off a light switch, the fish stopped biting. Dad speculated that there might be some larger fish that had just swam into the area to feed and had their smaller counterparts all spooked. Maybe it was a snake, or otter, or beaver, possibly. We waited and watched, all our lines still in the water, for some explanation, or at least for the intruder to pass. Dad was the first to spot the spiny patch appear on the surface, just behind a pair of glassy eyes. It was an alligator. A very small one, as alligators go, probably no more than two and a half feet long, but an alligator, nonetheless. It managed to keep just enough distance from the boat to ensure its own safety, but close enough to share in our dinner find. Disappearing for moments at a time, then resurfacing in a different spot, the small intruder managed to keep us from getting a single bite, all the while piquing the interest of a curious six-year-old.

Boredom, increasing heat from the rising sun, and pure mischief, I guess, finally got the best of me. With each cast of my faithful rod, I inched closer and closer to the harmless-looking little lizard, floating, now, much closer to our boat. One final cast placed a hook, sinker, and plastic float just inches beyond my target. As the line settled across his back, the startled alligator lunged away from my approaching cast and straight into my hook. I had seen it on television – Tarzan movies, I think – but never knew that alligators actually rolled over and over to escape their captors. They do. He did. With a tug on the end of my line, the only natural instinct that I knew was to pull back, dragging the panic-stricken alligator closer and closer as he tangled himself into my line, rolling and flailing for all he was worth. Panic had also set in, by now, among my three fishing partners. All offering instructions at once, one louder than the other, they failed to realize that their fishing lines were all still in the water. After retrieving all the lines within reach of his current position, the alligator decided to dive beneath the boat, surfacing on the other side to gather the remaining group into the tangle. We now sat with all our hooks embedded into a nest of fishing tackle, attached to a most unhappy, and, I must say, unpleasant reptile.

Dad, to the rescue, grabbed a pocket knife out of the tackle box and began cutting the lines to free them from further disaster. As he reached the final line, still held taunt by my Zebco "'33," the intruder surfaced once more, this time just three feet from the end of my rod. With all the strength he could muster, fueled by passionate frustration, Dad landed the edge of a boat paddle near the center of the alligator's back. Relatively unharmed, yet now aware of his release from the recent tether, he quickly chose deeper water over the risk of further abuse and was never seen again. Needless to say, with our guest now departed, I became the center of attention. The look on my dad's face assured me that the boat paddle, still in his hand, might prove itself to be of further use. For whatever reason, though, my duly earned punishment went un-administered.

Somehow, Dad had a natural sense of distinguishing between childish mischief and downright meanness. Thankfully, he got this one right. Even so, my six-year-old wisdom prompted me to offer no further suggestion or advice regarding the situation, or even to request a much-needed repair to my line. Fishing was over for the morning.

Despite the lack of corporal punishment that I had anticipated, I did manage to learn a lesson or two. Lesson #1: Never tease an alligator. They are not known to respond very well. Lesson #2: Size does not matter when it comes to alligators. Small or large, "gators are gonna be gators." Their habits do not change, they all respond to aggravation the same way, and the consequence of messing with one is always a disaster. Final lesson: <u>Whatever</u> you do, don't attempt to drag one into the boat with you. That tends to make <u>everyone</u> unhappy.

I have had occasion to meet up with a number of alligators in my life since that day – some large and some small - most of which I had sense enough to leave alone. There always seems to be something in my path, appearing harmless enough, that arouses my curiosity. My generation led a sheltered life compared to today's standards. About the most trouble, a person could get into back then pales by comparison to the morning headlines. The temptation to experiment with alcohol or drugs was a prominent cultural trend as I entered high school. Even still, there were hardly any laws in place to deal with these new-found curiosities, and still no track record of consequence for society to condemn the actions. Family values were the prominent guiding authority, and, for the most part, sufficient. Little did we know the profound toll that drugs and alcohol abuse would take over the next decade – seemingly harmless enticements that would entangle children, adults, marriages, and lives, into inescapable messes.

Today's news briefs us, daily, on the shootings, arson, gang violence, murders, and sexual offenses – often among elementary and middle school students. A chill rolls down my spine as I dare to think of what new "gators" will enter the scene as temptations as my grandchildren, and even their children, come behind me. The invasion of the home computer into nearly every home has introduced the lowest elements of humanity to children young enough to still require the help of a stack of phone books to reach the keyboard. Perhaps worse is the isolation that the contraptions have created, often finding every family member in their own world, staring for hours into a monitor, oblivious to the other people and relationships around them.

Should we, then, all throw our computers out the window in unison? Well, that may be a little overboard. But we should be prepared to recognize a predator when it enters our home. The wolf no longer comes to our door disguised as a sheep. We learned that trick. He is more likely to show up looking like the friendly neighborhood dog, man's best friend – or maybe a laptop, cell phone, video game, or iPad.

I can't help but draw a parallel between invasions into the lives of today's children with the increase in divorce, child abuse, and the general deterioration of the traditional family unit. My parents knew a "gator" when they saw one. They made it a point not to let one in the house. When my curiosity became likely to overcome their caution, they reinforced their stand with whatever means that was required, boat paddle in hand. They were relentless in their pursuit of teaching me to identify harm in my path and avoiding it, instead of allowing the consequence of experimenting to teach me. The scrapes and bruises that come with learning to ride a bike on your own are one thing. The bite of today's "alligators" is yet another.

As a result, though it took years of growing up, I have come to recognize the value of my parents' experience and now depend on it often for direction. We certainly cannot return to ideas and activities of a lifetime back, simply because they were effective then, but maybe it would not hurt to revisit the ***ideals*** of yesterday – time-tested, proven principles, guaranteed to maintain a moral standard for the future. Parental responsibility is a good start. An occasional fishing trip couldn't hurt, either – without an I-Pad or cell phone along for company.

nine

O.K., that is enough time spent on solving the world's moral problems – <u>way</u> too serious. Back to the vacations. Even the most basic of family vacations were memorable, somehow. Looking back, it seems the simple aspects of my childhood are the ones that now stand out. Toys, for example. One Christmas brought a bicycle, one a go-cart, and yet another, my first shotgun (still have it). But of all the things I spent time playing with, my favorites were the ones my dad made for me. A block of wood and a pocketknife in Dad's hands could conjure the most imaginative little car or truck. My very favorite was an airplane – sanded smooth and fitted with wings and tail section – even a propeller that would spin in the wind. It is possible that the finances of the day prompted the construction of these simple playthings, rather than their purchase. No matter, I treasured them as though they were fashioned from pure gold, not so much for their quality, but because Dad had made them especially for me. He always had a talent for making the simplest of gestures into some of the most meaningful of life. His sincerity and love showed in everything he did. He never trivialized my needs, or wants for that matter, and certainly not my dreams.

Kevin had just turned three and had already shown tremendous talent in the area of construction. He had a fascination with how things worked, how they were assembled, and what was inside of them. It was all too evident that we would never be able to deter him from taking things apart, so we set about teaching him how to re-assemble those things that he so ably scattered into oblivion. Christmas was just around the corner and Dad decided to do his part to aid the training. Among the clothes and other "necessity" gifts that grandparents are famous for, Kevin discovered two new screwdrivers – Craftsman – good ones – and a block of wood with half a dozen screws protruding about halfway out, in a variety of shapes and sizes. The idea was to teach him to take them out, then put them back, using the proper tool. I have no recollection of any other gift that Kevin received that year. I am sure there were many. He certainly had no interest in anything else for weeks to come. It wasn't long until Kevin could not only remove and replace the screws but could do so no matter how tightly they were installed. It might take a little longer, sometimes, but he would not be defeated. Just like any man with a handful of tools, he learned, also, to apply whatever tool he had, to whatever job was at hand. A screwdriver makes a good wood chisel, pry bar, can opener, paint stirrer, or scraper. They are versatile instruments when the need presents itself and the proper instrument is not available. A good Phillips head screwdriver even makes a good drill . . . for punching holes . . . especially in drywall, it seems . . . in Dad's living room wall. I can still see the smile on his face as he seemed to actually enjoy patching the results of Kevin's ingenuity. After all, giving a three-year-old a screwdriver was just asking for it. Though Dad never turned his back on Kevin with tools present again, he never took them back, either. The lessons learned by both had proven much too valuable to discard them now.

Back at home, things were not much different. Within a week of Christmas, I entered the kitchen from the foyer only to have the kitchen door knob fall off in my hand. Kevin stood on the other side with a pair of screws in his hand and an amazing attempt at offering a three-year-old explanation as to why they needed removing. I assisted with their replacement. Not two days later, the same knob fell loose once again. As I pulled open the door in search of our resident junior carpenter, the whole door nearly fell off of the frame. Kevin had not only removed the knob, but the screws holding the lower hinge in place as well. This second instance required a little sterner instruction, but, taking a queue from Dad, I let him maintain possession of his prized tools, but made **him** replace both the knob and the hinge. He did so proficiently and with a look of accomplishment on his face that remains printed on my brain. Since <u>he</u> had been the one to re-install the door and the knob, there never seemed to be a reason to remove it again. He did manage to investigate the inner workings of every toy in his collection that had a screw aiding its assembly. Some went back together, while others did not survive. Each, in its own way, served its owner well, even in demise.

With the pair of screwdrivers now resting in plain view on top of his toy box, and slightly out of reach of his bed, Kevin seemed resolved to settle into the night's rest – finally. Overhead light out, and nightlight on, Linda and I ventured back to the main level of our split-level home to enjoy the company of our television, and of one another.

Kevin and I had already begun to develop a mental connection of some sort – a strong one – that I am at a loss to explain completely. We seem to think just alike. We often finished one another's thoughts or sentences. About thirty minutes after putting Kevin down for the night, and he now "surely" sound asleep, the lights in the living room flickered . . . once, then again. I instantly sprang to my feet and headed for the hall, clearing the six steps leading to the upper-level bedrooms, touching down only once and scaring Linda half to death. I was not nearly so frightening, though, as the scene that waited around the corner in Kevin's room. How I knew, well, it's just that "mental" thing between the two of us.

Kevin's bed was low, for his easy access, and pushed up against the outside wall of his bedroom. I had never given a minute's consideration of the electrical outlet located squarely in the middle of the wall alongside his bed. The nightlight's dim glow had provided ample light for Kevin to retrieve his screwdriver set and remove – first the outlet cover, then the screws holding the outlet in place, and finally, the drywall within six inches of the outlet box perimeter. Applying, once again, his creative use of available tools to the task at hand, he found the screwdriver useful in prying the outlet completely out of the wall. As the outlet exited its protective box, the screwdriver had contacted the bare power wires causing a short, and the flicker in the lights. Buying the best quality tools really came in handy this time. The heavy insulation offered by the handle of that Craftsman screwdriver may actually have saved Kevin's life. I don't know if I was more frightened or relieved as I listened to another jabbering defense of the events just past. I repaired the outlet to a reasonable point of safety and, this time, placed the screwdrivers out of reach. Sorry Dad. There has to be limits. Thank God for insulation, anyway, when we can find it.

ten

a random thought . . .

I bought a Corvette. A yellow one. Not a new one, mind you. In fact, it is a fairly old one – 1978 – now nearly 30 years old, at the time of purchase. The car is in good shape, and I have always wanted one. I bought it as a present for myself for my 55th birthday

Funny thing about gifts that you buy for yourself – all of the enthusiasm is truly local. I quickly learned that no one else was as excited about it as me. I expected them to be at least happy <u>for</u> me, if not <u>with</u> me. No one was particularly **unhappy**, you understand – most hardly cared at all. Anyone who *did* bother to offer an opinion also questioned the need, or the color, or the age, or even what I intended to do with it. Now, any Corvette owner – if they are truly honest – will tell you that no one actually *needs* such a vehicle – it is purely a matter of *want*. As to the color and the age, those were personal choices. I like it – that is why I bought it. And what to <u>do</u> with it? You don't <u>do</u> **anything** with it. You just *have* it, and *drive* it, and *look at* it, and *clean* it, and *enjoy* it. All the puzzled looks that

I got told me that I was never going to sell that argument. Linda's primary objections to my choice of toys come on three fronts – 1- It has only two seats, 2- It does not have a trunk, and 3- it is too fast. Oddly, I have discovered that those are exactly the three main reasons I enjoy the car as much as I do. It does have only 2 seats, so I have no obligation to carry people around, or pick up anyone. It's just me, and maybe the one person I enjoy spending my private time with the most, when I can talk her into actually getting in it. The lack of a trunk means the vehicle is not suited for trips to the grocery store, or the mall, or especially to Wal-Mart, (**_ESPECIALLY_** Wal-Mart) because there is just no room to put the endless amount of stuff invariably generated from trips to places of that sort. Finally, as for the speed, I am not sure there is actually such a thing as too much power from a car. But even a ridiculous amount of horsepower does mean that you *have* to drive fast - just knowing that you could if you wanted to, is satisfaction enough. I guess that's just a guy thing.

I have heard a variety of learned and respected people say that you can never depend on other people to make you happy; you have to find happiness within yourself. As a general rule I have found human beings to be the least reliable life-form on the planet, and rarely put much stock in any of their promises, intentions, or opinions. Still, I do enjoy involving other people in the things that make me smile. I guess, more than I realized, I actually needed the validation of family and friends as much as I wanted the car. It was all part of the experience of doing something totally out of the ordinary for me; something that I had long wanted to do. The validation I sought did not come.

I still love the car. It was a huge check on my "bucket" list. I feel good about myself when I am in the car and have no regrets about my purchase. It sounds a little selfish, I know, but the things I have done – just for me – since then have been just for me. I am still willing to share, but I am no longer dependent on the endorsement of anyone else for my satisfaction.

I got a call from a very good friend this afternoon. Stanley wanted to show me his new truck. Though already near retirement age, Stanley had probably never owned a newer vehicle in his life. This was a one-owner, last year's model, with very low miles.

You could hear the smile in his voice as he proudly displayed his beautiful, blue, four-door dream, leather seats and all. I listened carefully as he told the whole story of his search and negotiation. He demonstrated the truck's more notable features, still in awe of his newly acquired treasure. I assured him that he had made one of the best deals imaginable, and that I envied his remarkable find. I raved about the abundant features, perfect paint, and clean interior. I passed off the chip or two in the truck's bed lining as perfectly normal and hardly noticeable. Validation was in order. Offering it was the very least I could do. It did not hurt me a bit. What's more, I was truly, genuinely, glad to share in his joy. Stanley will probably have his truck for a long time to come – and love it.

update. . .

I have had my Corvette for a little over two years now and have driven it a total of about three hundred miles. I enjoyed every mile immensely. It has served its purpose well. I sold it today, for exactly what I paid for it. Still no regrets, and perhaps, someday, I will own one again.

eleven

I used to be pretty good at book reports and such. How can this "book writing" thing be that much different? I wrote a short story or two, essays, and the like – short bursts of creativity – when I was in high school. But that was a <u>long</u> time ago, and never a book. I wrote a poem once. That's it – poetry! Maybe I can put some of Mrs. Stokes' lessons on iambic pentameter to use. I did write one poem - the day before my daughter's wedding. I gave it to her that night, and, as far as I know, no one else has ever read it. I remember the title; let's see how much of the poem I remember . . .

All Dressed In White

All dressed in white, that tiny gown,
With lace and ribbons stitched around.
Just two days old - just starting out -
In Mama's arms, with Daddy – proud.
Sleeping days, awake at night,
Routines to learn, fatigue to fight,

But when at last we're offered rest
The end of day recalls the best
And disregards the toil and fears,
Now hopeful that our dear Lord hears
Our prayers for help in days to come.
Thankful for this precious one.
A few days in and now it seems
That life thus far was just a dream.
And now there's purpose for my soul -
This precious gift, just two days old.

All dressed in white, that tattered shroud
With stains and stitching coming out.
With play clothes now all stored away;
No time for play this somber day.
If only I could take the place
Of this small miracle of grace.
If only I could stand this ground
And don instead this hospital gown.
A minor fix, "routine" they say
But worries still invade the day.
Time seems still – forevers pass –
Tears and worries, hard to mask.
Just hours hence, we were to see,
There's little to recovery.
Awake, then up, then out of bed,
Then down the hall, this toddler sped
In search of new adventures bold,
Amazed at what life next would hold.
And all the while I stood amazed
At God's great hand at work today.
I stopped to ponder that small dress
And wondered if God chose to bless
Others who had worn it first
Or those who would employ it next,
Or would He choose to take them home,
Leaving parents on their own

*Without the blessings, I now knew.
I prayed for them, not knowing who.*

*All dressed in white, a satin gown,
Four-cornered hat, my princess crown.
Before I blinked, years passed away,
It's kindergarten graduation day.
Songs to sing, artwork to see,
Then suddenly it occurred to me
A minor milestone had been passed,
Pathways set, futures cast.
Some friendships made would last through life.
But what of me? Amid the strife
Of learning life's demanding race
Would she still wish to seek my face
And ask just how she should proceed,
Or then my thoughts no longer need?
Two more crowns – four corners each -
Are milestones yet that she would reach
And each day I have to let go
One more small part of her, I know.
I give her not to this world's snares
But commit her life to God's kind care
To keep her safe when I'm not there;
Show her His path and hold her near.*

*All dressed in white, a silky gown.
More lace, more ribbons, flow to the ground.
Though tiny, still, she is not yet grown.
A wedding dress, though not her own.
Her task at hand – to lead the way
For another on this wedding day.
By dropping petals, one by one
To lead the way for one to come.
A perfect picture of someday
When she herself would pass this way.
My role would be to pass her hand*

> To another, stronger, younger man
> To care for her as I had tried,
> To love her, keep her by his side.
> I bowed my head and asked in prayer
> To spare me so I might be there
> Just long enough to see her grown
> With spouse and blessings of her own.
>
> Though years would pass with blinding speed
> The memories of her every deed
> Now grace each day of humble life
> Help ease the stress, the pain, the strife.
> Now looking back, it's plain to see
> Those years of growing up to be
> The woman she has now become
> Were fleeting jewels, lived but once.
> She learned from me, in small amounts,
> Things she should do —what life's about.
> But more than she, it's me who grew.
> She helped *me* learn what *I* should do.
> My list of failings on the way
> Are inked in journals for each day.
> At God's own hands as he writes there
> My sins committed my lack of care.
> Yet pages past have been erased
> Forgiven by His lasting grace
> And though I'll never understand
> How I, this humble, sinful man
> Deserve this gift, this breath in me,
> This little girl He sent to me,
> I thank Him daily for her there
> And lift her up each day in prayer.
>
> All dressed in white, a floor-length gown
> With train, bouquet, and veil for a crown,
> Showed proof that God had answered prayers
> And granted now my presence there.

My role that day, to give away
That precious gift on this, their day.
And so I will, with joy and tears
Release her hand, despite my fears.
And someday should she chance to find
The need for help, or just some time
To share her pains, or fears, or joys,
I hope that God would grant, once more
To me, this humble, grateful man,
The chance to stand and hold her hand
And be the Dad mine was to me
And point her focus upwardly
To view the face of One whose arm
Can shield her from all this world's harm
Whose love, its true, forever lasts,
Whose tenderness is unsurpassed.
And when my time on earth is done
With all life's battles, lost or won,
And by her side no more I stand
My God, and hers, will take her hand.

After reading the poem, Wendy questioned "How in the world did you remember all those details?" It is impossible to explain to anyone who does not have kids of their own, let alone not yet even married, just what a role children play in your lives. She was the first thing that I had ever encountered that truly occupied my mind, 24 hours a day, seven days a week. There were no breaks, no vacations, no relief, and strangely, no desire for any, from the responsibility that came with this new intrusion. When Kevin came along, it was no different. I now lived for no other reason than to monitor every detail of both their daily lives. I do not have to *remember* those scattered events; they are the very fabric of my life.

Wendy now has Morgan and Kalen at the center of her own attention. Kevin is the Dad to Drew and Paisley. Just ask them how they manage to remember so much about their children.

twelve

OK, concentrate. THINK, THINK, THINK! This book writing is not going to get the best of me. I can do it. What I need is a little of Dad's patience. Patience, patience, patience. Just calm down, and relax, and the ideas will come. Patience ....
....
....
.... Alright, so much for patience! I'm tired of waiting! Just start typing. *Now is the time for all good* . . . oh, good grief. How pathetic. Maybe I *can't* do this.

Now just listen to me. I'm talking myself into failure. I would never allow my kids to use "I can't" as an excuse. My kids. Maybe that could be the answer. No, not a book *about* them – a book *for* them – and *their* kids as well; a book about their grandparents and great-grandparents. Everyone ought to know at least a little bit about their ancestors. Mom and Dad have been trying to teach me a little more about mine. It is hard to believe that life has changed so much in just a few short years. I did a little math and discovered that my grandmother, Mom's mother, was already twenty years old when women got the right to vote. Dad's mother lived as a child somewhere west of the Mississippi River in, what is now, Oklahoma. It was Indian territory then – not even a state.

My great-grandfather (Dad's grandfather) was a combination blacksmith and coffin maker. Of course, everyone did at least a little farming, and raised a little livestock, just to feed the family. Money was a minor, and scarce, commodity. Goods and services were more often traded for than bought. He and his family learned great respect for the Indians whose homes and land surrounded theirs. Both generally kept their distance – their lifestyles were so different. Still, there was no room for prejudice on either part. Life was hard for all. They simply learned to live together, peacefully, and even lend an occasional hand

My grandmother was very young, just barely school-age at the time. If life was not tough enough, winter in their neck of the woods could be brutal at times. The school was a couple of miles away. It is hard to imagine sending my own six- or seven-year-old daughter out the door, just about daylight, to walk a couple of miles to school on her own. Nonetheless, such was the norm. Everyone attended the same school, in the same class, no matter their age. Grandma's class had even attracted a couple of Indian children, including one teenage boy who lived close by, but a little farther from school than she. His age was a little hard to determine, but his stature was certainly that of a nearly grown man. One winter morning, the family woke to find a blanket of fresh snow on the ground. The routine was the same, good weather or bad, so preparation began for the daily trek to school. Just as Grandma prepared to leave, there came a knock at the door. Everyone was surprised to see the Indian boy standing at the door. My grandmother knew him, from school, of course. Without a word, he motioned toward the road outside, and my grandmother exited the house with goodbyes to everyone. Much to her surprise, as her feet touched the top step, the large visitor reached down, still silent, and picked up my grandmother with one arm and swung her onto his back. There she rode until they both arrived safely at school. The return trip that afternoon was the same. Every morning after that, whenever inclement weather prevailed, the young man showed up and carried my grandmother the two miles to school. It was hard not to befriend such an unsolicited sacrifice

Come spring and a welcome break in the weather, great-granddad decided to put his carpentry skills to use, helping to build a church in the community. Such a building would, no doubt, serve as a church, a school, the town hall, and any other use that presented itself. Often, one of the first buildings erected in a new settlement, it would serve as the centerpiece for gatherings – by Indians and newcomers alike. Everyone pitched in, with both labor and materials, until the main structure was finally under the roof. A large bell had been ordered, no doubt from somewhere back along the east coast. Its' long-awaited arrival now presented the arduous task of hoisting it into the bell tower on top of the church and securing it in place. Ropes, pulleys, and all the manpower they could collectively muster slowly coaxed the bell toward its' new home. Great granddad was perched atop the tower, guiding the bell into place, ready to tie it off and secure the weight. With only the last few inches to go, the unexpected changed his life forever. A timber supporting most of the bell's weight suddenly snapped and allowed the bell to slip.

Great granddad reached out, over his head and grabbed the bell to steady it, keeping it from crashing down on the other workers below. With all the strength he could summon, he managed to hold the bell still, wedged against the bell tower wall, until additional ropes were brought up and the bell temporarily secured. The avoided injuries to those working below, thanks to his swift reflex action, were paid for at a high personal cost. Though he managed to hold the bell, the strain of the weight ruptured an artery in his heart. Even able to determine the probable extent of the damage, the medicine of the day offered no repair. He survived, at home, for another two years. He was able to do little more than get around the house on his own. The heavier work went, mostly, undone.

Fall arrived and brought a decided chill to the air. It was time to slaughter the hogs that great-granddad had raised for meat to span the winter. But his health had only grown worse, and Great Grandma was not capable of such a physical task. The children were all still much too young. The family drifted to the tides of whatever life sent their way, whether hardship or the occasional generosity of a neighbor. Early one morning, Great Grandma awoke to the sounds of voices and the squealing of a couple of pigs. She awakened her husband, informing him of the racket coming from the fenced lot outside. From the back window, they were able to see several horses, recognizable as those ridden by the local Indians – white with brown and black patches, and blankets for saddles.

Now there may well have been a developing respect between Indians and white settlers moving west – even an occasional friendship here and there; but the reputation of one in the eye of the other still dictated a certain amount of suspicion and a general mistrust. Great-granddad had little reason to worry about the morning visitors. Still, this was an unusual intrusion, and his failing health provoked a helpless feeling that he was about to fall victim to those surely there to steal their hogs. Unable to defend his property, or even himself, and resolved to his plight, he told great grandma that there was simply nothing that either of them could do. He could only let the Indians take the hogs and hope they would leave without further harm. But, for some reason, the intruders seemed in no hurry to get away. The activity around the pen continued for some time until, finally, the squealing hogs were silenced. Still, there was no attempt at a hasty retreat.

The family watched, afraid, yet amazed, as the team of suspected robbers began methodically cleaning, skinning, and cutting up one hog after another. With the last one neatly dressed out and cleaned, the Indians began carrying the slabs of meat across the yard to great-grandad's smokehouse, where they hung the meat – every piece – to cure for the winter. They then disappeared back into the woods, without a word, as quietly as they had arrived. Immeasurable gratitude now replaced the fears of earlier in the morning. Though different in so many ways from him, my great-grandad's native neighbors recognized a need, suffered by a fellow man, and responded. Great-granddad died the following year from his injuries.

I cannot help but be touched by the comradery that developed between two very different peoples. Often staying at arm's length from one another, they always came together when either needed the other. It seems the hardships of the day served as their common ground. So many years later I was privileged to grow up without such primitive conditions, yet people groups of my day (and even now) have such difficulty finding common ground, even though we are more alike than ever before. As a young boy I can remember visiting my doctor whose office boasted two separate entrances – one labeled "white" and the other labeled "colored". Black patients often waited until all the white patients were taken care of before they were attended to. Water fountains and public restrooms were duplicated as well, each bearing the same labels of separation.

I sat on a public transit bus, the driver refusing to move, until the black patrons who entered moved to the rear of the bus to be seated – at the driver's direct instruction. I witnessed the race riots of the '60s. I went to high school with someone whose father was head of the local KKK. I have seen crosses burned in family's yards. It was not until my senior year of high school that I saw anyone of color in any of my classes. Even then, only a small handful of black kids were enrolled in my school. Most of them did not want to be there, but their parents were paid – by the NAACP or other civil rights groups – to put their children there. "Bussing" became the buzzword for equal rights, where black children were picked up at home by county school buses, sometimes before 6:00 in the morning, and transported as much as an hour or more away to an all-white school. No one benefited. That was a long time ago and things have changed. I am not sure they have changed for the better, just different. I have to ask – if our ancestors were able to muster so much compassion for one another based on the harsh conditions of their lives, how is it that we can remain in such contempt of one another as we all enjoy the richest life the world has to offer?

thirteen

Along with a proud legacy, my great-grandfather passed along at least one piece of evidence that represented his superb blacksmithing skills. It was a .22 caliber, single-shot, rifle that he had made by hand for my grandmother. It featured an octagonal barrel, and steel sights, and was scaled to fit my grandmother's petite frame. Even today's modern firearms would find difficulty in matching the accuracy fashioned into this, my grandmother's prized possession. That accuracy, coupled with her skill as a marksman, was evident to my own dad, as he would later sit on the banks of the Chattahoochee River and watch his mom take target practice. She would toss sweetgum balls into the water and shoot them as they floated downstream. Notice, I said shoot them, not try to shoot them. A target just smaller than a golf ball, bobbing and bouncing along in the swift river currents was a worthy adversary of the most skilled of shooters with the finest of equipment. It fell victim, nonetheless, to the keen eye of a strong young woman with a handmade rifle.

When talk of western settlements before statehood, Indians, and one-room schoolhouses begins to seem like ancient history (or at least a Saturday afternoon with Zane Grey), I must remind myself that I actually knew my great-grandmother. I was very small when she died, but I do recall seeing her on our Sunday afternoon visits to my grandmother's house, sitting in her favorite chair, as the entire family would gather for our weekly visits. She had earned the right, I suppose, to be as cantankerous as she pleased and certainly displayed the well-practiced trait with pride. I can't ever recall seeing her without a can of snuff by her side, easily within reach on the table by her chair. On her other side, on the floor, was a coffee can – the receptacle for her expelled tobacco. Her aim was generally good, though the floor around the can showed evidence of an occasional distraction. To make matters worse, there was no refusing a hug from each child who entered, no matter the smell, or the floor, or even a little stain leaking from the corner of her mouth. The scene has remained etched in my mind until this very day and has served as an ample deterrent to my own experimentation with tobacco.

My grandmother lived on to raise seven children. The eighth one died at only a couple of years old. With all of the children finally out of the house and on their own, she enjoyed a long career in the bakery of The National Biscuit Company, or Nabisco, as it is known today. Following her retirement, I was privileged to spend many long summer afternoons fishing with her and my grandfather, listening to stories of their childhood and their upbringing. Fishing was the one pastime my grandmother preferred, even more than eating, if given the choice. A cane pole with a cork float seemed to always produce the most success. As was the story of her life, it was simple but trustworthy and effective.

My grandfather made his living as an automobile mechanic. He had no formal training in the field, but few did in his day. He ran his own shop, most of the time, and always managed to provide for his family. Provisions were modest, at times, but there was always food on the table. Oftentimes it was food taken on an afternoon hunting trip as opposed to a trip to the grocery store. Though I never had the opportunity to hunt with my grandfather, I am told that he was an excellent shot as well. He owned just one gun in all of his life – a single-shot, 12-gauge, shotgun. It was a common practice for the local hardware store to raise a little extra money by raffling off some sort of prize from time to time, often a gun. The process was sort of a cross between bingo and the lottery. The store kept a card with a series of numbers printed on it, each perforated so they might be punched out individually. For 25 cents, a customer was allowed to take a number from the "punch card". When all the numbers were sold, a drawing was held, and the person holding the winning number was awarded the prize. My grandfather bought four "punches" on this occasion, one of which netted him the gun – a pretty good investment for just a dollar. As for his proficiency with the weapon, Dad tells stories of my granddad's frequent afternoon trips into the woods near their home. These excursions were always labeled as "hunting" trips, though, everyone knew that a moon-shine liquor still could not tend to itself. Once in a while a little "maintenance" was necessary there, as well. Often, my grandfather would gather his gun and hat as he asked "Florida, how many rabbits you gonna need for dinner?" The reply would come back from my grandmother, "Oh, five will do, I guess." With that, and a serene confidence in his demeanor, my grandfather would pick up five shotgun shells and drop them into his pocket as he headed out the door. A couple of hours later, he would return, bearing dinner – five plump rabbits, as requested.

    With all of the time he spent hunting, duck hunting in particular was not his forte. He was often invited to go, by friends or family who lived for the sport, but the idea of a freezing morning, before daylight, in a boat in some swamp, was just not for him. On one occasion, after much persistence, he finally gave in to a duck hunting invitation. The damp, cold, dark morning was no disappointment to his expectations, nor was the boat or the swamp. After a few hours of waiting, and shivering – damp and disgusted with his waisted morning, without a single bird in sight, the hunting party decided to give up and search for a warmer spot, some dry clothes, and something to eat. Just as they turned to leave, a single duck was spotted, flying straight for the boat, about five feet above the water. My grandfather spotted the fowl, readied his gun, and slowly rose to his feet, balancing in the shallow boat, and drawing a bead on the duck. He waited until the very last moment to take his shot. Not unexpectedly, he centered the bird, killing it with ease on a single shot. Also unexpected was the weight and momentum of his prey, which had been approaching at full speed. The demise of the duck failed to deter its continued path, striking my grandfather squarely in the chest, and knocking him over backward into the lake. Ok, he had been duck hunting. Was everyone happy now? His first, and his last duck hunting trip was over.

Somehow the grass always seemed a little greener down the road to my grandfather, prompting him to move quite often, as the next job would entice him to wander from town to town and state to state. A house full of small children and the inconvenience of uprooting them was not enough to outweigh his need to press on.

One particular Friday afternoon, my grandfather came home from work and announced to the family that they should begin packing their belongings – he had taken a job out of state, beginning on Monday. There had been no discussion, no warning . . . they were just moving. My grandmother, though not unaccustomed to moving, insisted that there was no possible way that she could have everything, including furniture, ready to go with such short notice. And what were they going to do about the house? My grandfather was prepared with a simple answer. He calmly explained that the family need only pack their clothes and personal belongings. He had already sold the house and everything in it. There were no more questions. They simply moved. Again. This Nomad-Ish lifestyle led my father through thirteen different schools during only eleven years of education. Miraculously, he started and finished in the same school – the very same school, in fact, where I, myself, began and completed my high school years

My grandfather was not the only one who knew their way around a liquor still, (moonshine still) you understand. His brother-in-law, Uncle Luper was far more proficient, and far more profitable, in the moonshine business. What's more, he had a specialty in the trade – he made peach brandy. Though he operated a still in South Georgia – in the middle of nowhere – for years on end, he never got caught at it. Making homebrew was quite illegal and under the ever-watchful eye of the federal government. Their agents were well-trained at finding and destroying the most well-disguised and remote operations. The explanation for his success was simple – his best customer was the local sheriff. The sheriff bought more of Luper's brew than anyone and could not afford to have his primary source of refreshment shut down. From time to time, the sheriff would pull up to Uncle Luper's house and inform him, "Luper, the revenuers are Comin' at the end of the week – shut down the still." So, Uncle Luper would make his way out the path to his prized point of livelihood, gather up any brandy that had accumulated, and shut down the still so that its location would not be compromised by the trail of smoke coming from the cooker. He would then pack up, or cover up the main components, out of sight, and wait for the search to be over – once again informed by the sheriff that it was again safe to operate.

Dad's mom benefited as well from the family's questionable alcohol production, as did we all in one sense. If you ever thought there was such a thing as a "good tasting" Christmas fruit cake, then you can bet it was made by my grandmother. Somewhere just around Thanksgiving, she would start the process, making several cakes with a special method for storing them. The cake recipe was a fairly simple one, but it was the preparation that made them noteworthy. She placed each one in a metal cake canister, but just before snapping on the lid, she would wrap the cake in multiple layers of cheesecloth – soaked in homemade muscadine wine. Every week or so, she would crack open the lid and pour in another half cup or so of her secret ingredient, then reseal the container lid. By the time Christmas arrived, and time to cut the cake, when the lid was opened the aroma of the wine would literally take your breath. No one refused a slice of Grandma's fruit cake.

fourteen

As best anyone can recall, my grandfather made only two visits to a doctor's office in his lifetime, despite periods in his life when he was known to consume his fair share of alcohol, not to mention at least two packs of Camel cigarettes every day. The first visit was to Dr. Green for stitches in his leg. No small injury, he had been working under a car in his shop when it slipped off the jack supporting it. The car fell and landed on him, the fender cutting a gash in his upper leg from one side to the other. I doubt he would have bothered with a doctor, even then, if the normal remedy for such a malady had proven adequate. This time, however, just dousing the wound with a little Kerosene and wrapping it with a grease rag – a remedy that he had administered numerous times in the past - was not quite enough.

As time went on, his drinking, though never really a serious problem, subsided. Maybe it was the intimidating presence of thirteen grandchildren running around his place on Sunday afternoons that prompted the abstinence. Perhaps it was the occasional scolding from my petite, yet relentless, grandmother that finally straightened his path somewhat. But he never impressed any of us as someone to be "told' what he should or should not do.

His smoking, though a concern as well as an annoyance for much of the family, did not merit discussion. He turned a deaf ear and the first mention of his quitting. Still, one afternoon, without a word or warning (familiar pattern), from him, or anyone around, he reached into his shirt pocket and removed the half-full, soft-side Camel cigarette pack concealed there, and tossed it in the trash. He never smoked again, and never seemed to want another puff. No patches, no pills, no gum, candy, no nothing. No guilt trips or prodding. He just quit, cold turkey. I choose to believe that choices like that one stemmed from the same type of motivation as the need to move during his earlier years – he had finished with one phase of life, and it was now time for something else. Though I never moved more than 10 miles from my original home, still, it is easy for me to understand his independent attitude and choices.

I consider myself to have a fairly amiable personality; but it is, and always has been, impossible for anyone to make me do anything. I might easily be reasoned with or persuaded, but the more you prod and insist, the more determined I become to prove my resilience. Maybe my streak of independence was inherited from my grandfather. Maybe, too, I can take a lesson from his later life – earlier in my own perhaps – in the value of yielding a little to those with my best interest at heart.

His second visit to the doctor came following a stroke. It was only a matter of days until he drifted into a coma. Though the stroke had inflicted substantial damage, his body was far from giving up. Over the next several weeks, despite a battery of tests, bags of I.V. fluids, and every imaginable effort to keep him comfortable, doctors were unable to make any improvement. With nothing further to do medically, the hospital transferred my grandfather to a wing of the hospital labeled "extended care". It was the section my grandmother referred to as the place "where they send you to die". Her assessment was, understandably, a bit cynical. Her prediction, nonetheless, was inevitably accurate. He survived, now, without a word, blink of an eye, or knowledge of his surroundings. He required twenty-four-hour care provided, in large part, by the family. The "family" at that point, had dwindled down to only three brothers who were willing, able, and sober long enough to take responsibility for his care. Dad seemed to assume the lion's share of hospital time, sometimes staying all day and all night without relief, only to return to work the next day . . . somehow.

It was nearing Christmastime. I have always thought that there should be some kind of "bubble" around special days that keeps pain away, if only for that brief holiday. For the first sixteen years of my life, it had been a tradition for Mom, Dad, and I to go out in search of a tree – a real one – together. It was usually a Friday or Saturday night, a couple of weeks before Christmas. As luck would have it, the night selected for the task often turned out to be the coldest and rainiest night of the year. We would search from one tree lot to the next, usually favoring those with signs indicating proceeds going to some charity or local organization in need of the funds. All had to agree on the selection, which was carefully bound and placed stump-first in the trunk of the car. Once home, despite my annual pleas to decorate it immediately, the tree would be placed outside in a bucket of water to let the limbs "settle out" (and put off Dad's dreaded task of dragging all the decorations out of the attic at such a late hour). Finally, a couple of days later, the three of us would devote an entire evening to lights and ornaments, tinsel, and garland . . . even strings of popcorn and aluminum foil balls. A single, five-pointed, lighted star crowned our efforts, and the result seemed more spectacular with each passing year. Not so, this year.

Christmas Day was less than two weeks away, and no sign of a tree, or any interest in scheduling my favorite annual ritual. There was very little I could do to relieve the sorrow or the fatigue I had come to recognize daily in my Dad. But I could, at least, help with some of the "chores" of the season. I made the pilgrimage around the local tree lots and, with the best effort I could muster, selected the family tree. Once home, I placed it in a bucket of water, as usual, and awaited my parents to return home.

At that point, I guess I was hoping that the sight of a Christmas tree, minus the task of its' blustery retrieval, might spark some interest in the season at hand. Mom and Dad were, indeed, grateful, but lacked the enthusiasm that I had sought. My grandfather's condition worsened, and Dad's hospital time nearly doubled. Between time spent at his father's side, and a small amount of time working, he was almost never home. When he was, it was to catch a little much-needed sleep and return again to his post. On Wednesday night, with Mom and Dad both at the hospital, I rummaged the attic for the all-too-familiar decorations and carefully completed the tree, mindful of Mom's annual instructions for placing the icicles precisely at the end of each branch, one at a time . . . this time, alone with the task. I wasn't feeling sorry for myself, mind you, and certainly not resentful of the attention that my grandfather now required. The feeling, instead, was one of helplessness – to either relieve my grandfather's suffering or to revive the spirit of the holiday absent from our home. The final step was to plug in the lights and stand back in admiration. I am sure that this tree probably appeared, to most, as festive as any year previous, but in my eyes, the tree stood in a dark shadow of my grandfather's suffering. I put away the empty decoration boxes, unplugged the lights, and went off to bed to pray for my grandfather's recovery.

    I visited my grandfather as often as I could, trying to encourage my grandmother as best I knew how. It had been three long months since his stroke. On the following Friday, I decided to make such a visit, early in the morning, prior to going to work. Dad had pulled an all-nighter and it had actually been a couple of days since I had seen him. There was no change in my grandfather, but my dad was truly beginning to show the strain. He was tired beyond imagination and worried – about his job, his dad, his mom, and me and Mom. I could not imagine how much longer he could survive under these circumstances without collapsing himself. I left the hospital and started down the sidewalk to my car, attempting to soak in all that was going on around me. With a sudden clarity that had before been missing, I understood the real need in the situation

    The doctors had all assured us that there was no possibility of my grandfather's recovery; it was only a matter of time. Just how much time remained uncertain. His heart was strong, and it could be quite some time before other vital functions began to fail.

But my grandfather was in good hands – I knew that. Not in the doctors' hands but in God's hands. His future was protected, but this life had left him miserable and depleted. Some would find my next prayer to be selfish, uncaring, and even morbid. Truthfully, the prayer I prayed on the sidewalk that morning was probably the most unselfish prayer I had ever prayed. I asked God to let my grandfather die. God graciously answered my prayer at 7:00 that evening.

fifteen

Christmas is the ultimate reality check. As a small child, I viewed Christmas as the "perfect" day of the year. Nothing ever went wrong – in the entire world. It was truly a (cliché) "magical day." It never rained – the weather was always bright and sunny. Everyone was happy and healthy. Family was definitely on their best behavior. Now, 40 some-odd years following my grandfather's death, I once again decorated our tree alone.

Aside from my grandfather's passing, I recall Christmases when Mom and Dad both had the flu – in bed for nearly a week. Another year, it was my turn for the flu. Dad's sister, Opal, lost her life in an auto accident one Christmas Day. News of a great uncle's death in Florida came just a week or so before the holidays. The first year I was not able to see my son and his family at Christmas Time was probably the hardest of them all. Christmas day is not a time for tears, yet ...sometimes…. This year it is Linda's Mom. She is just out of the hospital following a 17-day stay to repair a broken vertebra in her neck. The surgery went well – steel plates, rods, and screws attaching her skull, to bones, to other rods, already in place from four years earlier – went off without a hitch. It was a very serious surgery, to say the least, especially for an 83-year-old. Hospitals, however, have their own special routine of how to dole out medications, even those that you take at home regularly, on a strict schedule and dosage. They tend to experiment with the dosage part and administer them in random order, seemingly without any sort of schedule. When you suffer from COPD, high blood pressure, heart arrhythmia, stage four kidney failure, and lung cancer, as Shirley does, it takes 17 days to re-balance all that they messed up. The neck surgery was secondary by comparison.

At home, she is recovering nicely but requires a great deal of assistance. Linda is struggling to balance an abbreviated work schedule with supplying meals, making (and keeping) doctor's appointments, keeping the house straight for her mom and dad, doing their laundry, grocery shopping daily, balancing a checkbook, and even helping to change her mom's clothes. That leaves absolutely no time for herself, let alone Christmas. But that is exactly as it should be. That's right – as it should be. Don't misunderstand – all that is an unbelievable amount of work that no one really wants to take on. There could be no better wish than for parents to be able to care for themselves, without a child's daily involvement in every detail of their lives. But that is where reality comes in.

Life happens…even at Christmas. I was fortunate enough (yes fortunate) to be able to provide some care for my mom and dad just before they died – just the small things that, hopefully, improved their quality of life in the smallest ways. It was a distraction from everything I had planned to do. It took time – lots of time – and lots of effort. Just making decisions for them in areas where I had no experience, was mentally and physically exhausting. But now, it seems like I did so little. The time that I was able to spend with them has become the most valuable days of my life. The same will be true for Linda…. someday.

sixteen

more random thinking . . .

The grass is always greener, in my case at least, in the middle of the flower beds. I had this one spot on the lawn. I tried everything, but grass would simply not grow – no matter what. I plowed it up to loosen the soil. I added topsoil. I added fertilizer. I put in seed and more seed. I watered it. Nothing. The plot remained bare. All the while, I was spending about as much time trying to keep the grass *out* of the few flower beds I had in the yard as I did working on the rest of the lawn. Finally, it occurred to me: that maybe the problem was in growing *grass*. Just maybe something else would stand a better chance of survival in this rocky little pit of despair. A flower bed would look nice there – near the road, behind the mailbox, right beside the drive. That's it – flowers! It was worth a shot. Sure enough, with the least amount of effort, and a few bucks' worth of flowers, the new bright spot in my yard *this* spring was that former desert area that had been so uncooperative. By mid-summer, there was no stopping them, and I actually began to consider other potential areas for improvement, certain that my "brown thumb" had finally gained a tint of green.

I know that I should not have been surprised that the grass – Bermuda to be precise – began to creep into the edges of my flower bed. It is, after all, the very nature of Bermuda grass to invade. My total frustration came nearer the end of the season when I discovered that this little patch of rocks and aggravation was still the most prolific growth on my property. . ... but now it was covered in grass. Lots of it. Tall grass. Dark green grass running everywhere. Where the flowers *used* to be. They did not stand a chance as the choking carpet of Bermuda filled the space to overflowing. It figures. Come the fall, the remaining blooms faded, and I simply mowed the new resident crop to a level rug. It remains, to this day, the thickest patch of grass in my yard.

That little stubborn patch taught me a lesson that has saved me a lot of time and trouble since. For one, I now know how to grow grass just about anywhere, given a little time and some flower plants. It occurred to me, as well, that life often behaves in much the same manner. Understand, I have never been one to give up hope, or simply resign to the inevitable without a fitting fight. I firmly believe that a positive attitude and enough effort *can* change a predictably formidable outcome. But there are times when you know – you just know – that no matter how committed you are to your efforts, the end is going to be the same. It is within sight and there is no stopping it. It is at that point that I have learned to *plan* for what I know is coming, *while* I fight it. Giving up is not an option, but I find it foolish to be unprepared for a result that rests on your front steps, just waiting for it's time to come. It sounds like a contradiction of effort – resisting the inevitable while planning for it. But in the end, I come out on top either way. If I win my battle, I count my efforts as a success. If I lose, at least I tried, and I have a backup plan to deal with it. Grass is a reality. It grows best in flower beds. Plan on pulling it out on a daily basis, or plan on mowing it.

seventeen

Somewhere in the middle of my elementary school years, Dad decided to invest in a piece of lakefront property. Through his business travels he managed to run across High Falls Lake near Griffin, Georgia. It wasn't a large lake, but the fishing was presumed good and the distance from home was quite convenient. Being the conservative that he was, he decided to lease a lot, rather than purchase one, to see how much use we actually got out of it. Its' end-of-the-cove location did not offer much of a view, and the lot was overgrown with brush and briars. I can remember two or three trips to the lake, each one spent clearing more and more of the lot, just to be able to reach the water. If we ever did actually go fishing, I don't remember it. The adventure did not last very long, and Dad dropped the lease after the second year or so. The idea of having a piece of lake property returned several years later. Armed with the pitfalls of the first outing, Dad began searching for a little more "polished" plot, with some sort of living quarters in place. One Sunday afternoon, while scouring the newspaper "want ads," he ran across a place for sale on Lake Martin, in central Alabama.

The property included a small, furnished house, a boat dock, and a covered shed, all positioned on a leased lot. The lot was owned by Alabama Power Company and had nearly eighty years remaining on a one-hundred-year lease. The lot rent was around $50.00 per year and the asking price for the house - $25,500.00. Dad had made up his mind to buy the place before asking but wanted me to see it and offer an opinion. We drove down on a Sunday afternoon in the late Fall to have a look.

We made the journey without the first sighting of an interstate highway. I was certain it would be dark before we arrived. We ventured from main highways to back winding roads, to narrow gravel trails, and, finally, to a dirt drive, as Dad announced our arrival. I don't know if my experience from years before came back to mind, or if I had just been expecting more. Whatever the reason, all I could see from the road was the need for yard work, paint, and repair. The dock, the shed, the house, the yard – all needed work. Lots of work. The house had been built by Russell Mills, the primary employer and landholder in the area, for weekend use by the mill employees. Similar houses were scattered around the lake, all having been built some 30 years earlier. The inside was no less disappointing. The only bathroom had a metal-lined shower stall and a wall-mounted lavatory. Rust and mold were in plentiful supply. The kitchen cabinets were entirely makeshift with curtains for doors on the lower, and only, cabinets. The walls of the main living room and single bedroom were lined with dark, vertical pine paneling. A pair of window-mounted air conditioners were expected to provide comfort for the summer, with no accommodations for Winter whatsoever – not even a fireplace or wood stove.

The "furnishings" consisted of a few old pots and pans, mismatched glassware and flatware, and a couple of Army cots. Now I am no snob when it comes to roughing it, but the mold, mildew, rust, and bugs were insurance for me that a good cleaning was in order if not a good throwing-out before any overnight stay. Care was to be taken as you stepped out onto the (mostly) screened porch that faced the lake. And the lake! Where had it gone? The water level was 10 feet below the bottom of the dock and began no less than 30 feet away from the farthest corner. "They tell me the water will come up in the spring," Dad explained. I hated to doubt him, but there was no way the water level was going to rise that far in just a few months. Clearly, Dad was about to be taken to the cleaners. Despite my attempts to point out all of my misgivings, Dad's enthusiasm about the place would not be diminished. I do not recall offering a single encouragement about the place. When Dad finally asked the one question we had come to answer, all I could tell him was "buy it if you want, but don't do it for my sake – I am not interested." A few weeks later my father was the proud owner of a piece of lakefront real estate in Alabama, warts, and all.

The concept of having a place at the lake was somehow inviting despite the appearance of *this* particular place. But if I was to spend any time on a lake, I would have to have a boat. What good was 44,000 acres of water if I was able to enjoy only a few feet in front of the dock (if it actually ever returned)? As it happens, the former owner of the house had one of *those* for sale as well. It sat in a nearby storage shed, covered in a thick, two-year layer of red dirt. With less than 40 hours on the boat since purchase, and the asking price near half its actual value, I was sold. Nearly a full day of cleaning, a new battery, and some fresh gas proved my investment worthwhile. I unearthed (literally) a beautiful, 18' long speedster. The 115-horsepower outboard motor pushed this fishing/ski combination dream along the water at over 50 miles an hour. There was not a stitch out of place in the upholstery, not a sign of wear in the carpet, nor a scratch on the hull. The trim and tilt, live well pump, trolling motor and full instrument cluster all worked to perfection. I was hooked on life at the lake

The house was still a wreck. Over the next couple of years, Mom, Dad, Linda, and I set about to improve the place as best we knew how. Mom managed to clean the entire house within an inch of its life, and, with a few new dishes, some furniture and linens from home, and a little yard work, the place became nearly tolerable. Nearly. The one bathroom was of a quality only one notch above a backyard outhouse. I removed everything, down to the studs and replaced the tub, toilet, and vanity with modern equipment. When I tried to tie back into the existing plumbing, I found galvanized water pipe, iron gas pipe, plastic pipe, black drain hose, and even a garden hose used to link it all together. It all had to go. Armed with basic instructions from a friend who owned a plumbing supply business, more parts that I thought I might need, and ambition beyond my ability, I cut everything out and threw it into the yard. There was no turning back now. Over a couple of days that followed, I *learned* how to plumb a house from scratch. Surprisingly, it all worked.

One bedroom and one bath (remodeled though it was) were a constant problem, with only a cot, or sleeping bag for guests numbering more than two. We began discussing the possibility of additional rooms – bedrooms and baths particularly – finally deciding on a sketch that I had made. The new addition would include a second bedroom with closet space, an additional, shared bath, a place for washer and dryer, an expansion of the living area with windows along the back, and a stairwell leading to a storage room/future bedroom in the basement. Though a pretty big task altogether, it would be manageable if everyone helped out, and none of us were afraid of the work. Without any timeframe, or deadline to meet, we could take our time and finish out the space as money, and enthusiasm would allow. The first task was to remove the one portion of the house in the worst shape – the rear screened porch. That did not prove to be much of a problem, as most of the support posts had begun to rot anyway, and *none* were anchored properly into the ground. A couple of claw hammers, one sledge, a pry bar, and a single Saturday, and Dad and I managed to convert a rickety old porch into a pile of firewood alongside the house. This was going to be easy. Saturday evening took us back home, as usual, putting us back in place for Sunday church. It was Monday that changed everything.

Dad left for work, as usual, headed to his every-other-Monday-morning stop at Crescent Paint Company in north Atlanta, one of his largest customers. Arriving around mid-morning, he began his routine of coffee, conversation, and finally, a little inventory review and order-taking. His routine was interrupted though as he began to notice a discomfort along his left arm. It quickly escalated into pains in his chest and arm, nearly to the point of unbearable. Crescent Paint's owner immediately summoned one of his warehouse managers to take Dad to nearby Northside Hospital. No convincing was necessary, as by now, breathing was labored, and even walking unassisted was a struggle.

Mom got the call a little while later. She called Linda, who, in turn, called me at work. The two of them picked me up on the way, as we headed to check on Dad's condition. It was, in fact, a heart attack. The doctor described it as "moderate" with some damage to the left side of his heart. Time would tell just how much, but his timely arrival at the hospital had probably made a significant difference. A heart catheterization and one bypass surgery later, Dad survived, and the long, slow, recovery was to begin.

The heart attack kept Dad out of work for just over a month. It was that month that revealed more to me about who my father really was, and solicited more of my respect for him, than any other time in our lives together. Understand that his income was based solely on sales commissions. No work – no sales – no income. Three percent commission was small enough when business was good, but three percent of nothing was still nothing. Insurance covered the majority of medical bills, but at that point in his financial career, he was in no shape to survive a month without work.

Dad had a relationship with his customers that any salesman would envy. They were friends first, then customers. He often got into hot water with his sales manager when he refused to push the latest promotional product on customers whose market was not well suited for it. He forfeited rewards of his own – points, prizes, trips, money, and acclaim – for the wellbeing of his customers. He looked out for their businesses as though he were running them himself. He was often invited to go fishing, or out to dinner by one of those "friends" without the mention or concern for business. Dad genuinely enjoyed getting to know those people in his life who, ultimately, provided for our family. His friendship, and theirs, came without attachments, obligation, or expectation. The true definition of friendship was soon to be discovered. While lying in bed recovering, first in the hospital and later at home, an unorchestrated event in Dad's life would forever teach me the value of putting people and their needs above my own, and a lifelong respect for Dad's values.

Almost without exception, and without ever talking to one

another, Dad's customers began calling in orders to the main office. Not just small orders, mind you. Each and every one of his customers took stock of his warehouse and placed orders to max out their inventory for the month. Several even insisted that their thirty-day terms be waived, and the billing be done within the month, allowing Dad's commission to be paid within the month, as well. ***When all the counting was done, Dad's sales for the month broke all records for a single month by any salesman in the history of the company.*** The record stood for years and drew the attention of sales staff and management alike. Not bad for a month *out of work*.

I have to make one correction. I labeled this as an "unorchestrated" event. It was unexpected, but it was certainly not without design. You see, Dad's dependence on his income, his doctors, and even his family and friends, was listed well down the page below his dependence on God – in times of good health, or in the middle of a heart attack. It was God who had responded to the need. He used Dad's friends to do so – some who shared a trust in God, and some who did not. It was Dad who befriended his customers, in obedience to what he knew was right. It was his friends who became the tools of such a reward. But it was God's plan for his life that saw Dad through. He knew it and gave Him credit for it.

Dad taught me that same dependence. It has proven unfailing on countless occasions in my own life. Although I would never wish the first day of discomfort on my children or grandchildren, I hope I have been able to pass along to them the knowledge of God's care and concern for their lives, the fact that He has a plan for them, and the rock-solid dependence that is available at His feet. Their ability to successfully navigate the future hinges on it.

eighteen

As for the house at the lake, the porch was missing, the grading contractor had been scheduled to dig out the basement and pour the footings, and the blocks for the foundation were "on order." Dad would not soon be able to return to any such strenuous activity as this project would require. So, what do we do now? Finances had remained stable, as had Dad's enthusiasm for the project. Linda and I decided that we would take on the next step ourselves – framing the floor, walls, and roof. I ordered all the necessary framing for the floor and walls, borrowed a trailer from a friend, and hauled one enormous load of lumber to the lake. It would be a couple of months before I discovered that the oversized load and the long uphill pulls in getting that load in place would cost me a transmission in an all-too-light-for-the-job pick-up truck. A long weekend and Linda and I were able to put in the floor system and cover it with plywood. The next weekend produced the walls, and the next – with much-needed help from other family members – put a roof overhead.

The "space", at least, was complete. Windows, siding, and roofing were completed shortly thereafter, Dad was able to finally get back into the swing of things, if only on the lighter side. A year later it was hard to tell what the old structure had looked like. In the following years, county water (to replace the pump for the lake water supply), paving for the driveway, and a new dock would make appearances. A tornado that skirted the lake would prompt the necessity for more clearing of trees, brush, and debris, and would eventually create a reasonably manageable area for flowers, shrubs, and lawn. In all, twenty-one years of love would be poured into the improvement and enjoyment of this little postage stamp on the shore of Lake Martin. Four generations, thus far, had worked and played there, along with countless friends and relatives – many now passed on.

Each winter brought about the same routine for the lake house – cut off the water, drain the pipes, and, eventually, pull the boat home. With colder weather of late fall now beginning to set in, Dad and I were on just that one-day mission. I had not had as much time in recent years to spend at the lake as I would have liked. Work and church had occupied much of my time and left little to leisure. But I now had a business of my own and scheduling was somewhat easier. Linda had Fridays off, so we had planned to spend a little more time taking it easy and enjoying the water. Mom and Dad were still in good health, but taking care of his own home and trying to manage the place at the lake were beginning to take a toll, financially as well as physically. On the way home, Dad began talking about what he might eventually do with the lake property. He knew it was too much to keep up with. Even bringing the boat home was now safer, at least with my assistance. He caught me a little off guard when he announced that he and Mom had been talking about it and pretty much decided to sell the place. I knew the love they shared for the time they were able to spend there and knew, as well, how much they would miss the place. Purchasing it myself, for what it was actually worth, was out of the question, since the property values around the lake had, by this time, increased by nearly twenty times their original value. I suggested that he might consider renting out the place for a little extra income. The monthly expenses did eat into a, now fixed income, for sure, but the more we talked, the more I began to feel that the sale was not so much about the money as the work involved in keeping the place going. Before I had a chance to thoroughly explore the thought that crossed my mind, I began to hear the words come out of my own mouth. It almost seemed like someone else was talking as I made one other suggestion. Even if I could not swing a loan large enough to purchase the place for what it was worth, I could handle a monthly note, if Dad were willing to finance it. I made him a simple proposal – a business deal – with a few minimum requirements:

First, Dad would legally sell the house to me, free and clear for the total sum of one dollar – deed, title, lawyers, paperwork – the whole nine yards. The sale would include the house, property, furnishings, appliances, tools, boat – *everything*. Second, I would pay Mom or Dad a fixed monthly note (equal to about what they might rent the place for) for as long as either of them lived. Next, Dad was to keep a key and continue to use the house any way he pleased – come and go when he wanted, take his friends ... anything. Finally, it was to be understood that any expenses – utilities, repairs, taxes, improvements – were *my* responsibility.

Mom and Dad would be able to keep a place at the lake, without the expense or the responsibility. It seemed only right to me since that was the arrangement I had been afforded for all the years prior. I had been able to use the place as I wanted while they had carried the load. It was their turn to use the lake home without responsibility for a change. I had not even talked with Linda about this arrangement – one of the biggest decisions I had made since we were married - but was sure that she would agree. It just seemed so right. Dad insisted that I check with her, and he would do the same with Mom. Though I tried really hard to do so, I am not quite sure that I ever convinced either of them to treat my offer strictly as a business deal – I was not *asking* for the house but *offering* an alternative to selling it. If they needed the money from the sale, I was perfectly willing to let it go. Linda was in complete agreement. Mom liked the idea as well. A couple of conversations later between the four of us, we decided that everyone benefited – short-term and long – and drew up the paperwork. On January 11, 2002, Linda and I became the proud new owners of a house and property on Lake Martin.

Dad had certainly put in the lion's share of the work while he owned the place. He probably made the greatest changes in overall appearance, as well. But there was so much more to do as I picked up where he had stopped. The more costly parts were to come. A new refrigerator was first, followed closely by a sea wall, new dock, and boat ramp. I had the yard cleared and reshaped to control a swampy spot on the low side, then planted grass in place of the briars and poison ivy. Stairs to the house from the front drive, brick sidewalks, block retaining walls, and later, a brick patio would round out the exterior. Oh, and a new roof. Inside, I finished the basement bedroom, added a half bath, and began replacing all the windows with insulated vinyl. Central heating and air conditioning, at last, gave us the option to enjoy the lake occasionally through the winter, and much more comfortably during the summer.

Plans are constantly changing. A new project seems to crop up before I even have a chance to complete the current one. Everyone asks the same question – "When are you going to be finished with it so you can enjoy it for a change?" But I have come to find a completely different kind of enjoyment at the lake than most. I love the work. I love the design. I love the improvement. I love the change I am able to make with just my own effort. Some things I have hired others to do, but the ones that I am most proud of, the ones that mean the most, are those that I have completed with my own hands. As long as I am able to do so, I truly hope there is *always* some project waiting for me. Thank you, Dad, for ignoring my advice, so many years ago, and passing on this most valuable gem.

nineteen

2009 proved to be a particularly hard year. President Barack Hussein Obama was in office as President and was successfully undermining the U.S. economy; seemingly starting with me. Business slowed to nothing more than a trickle and I found myself relying on previous experience and training to earn a living. Remodeling, additions, and the like provided what little income there was – or would be, (as I was to later learn) for the next several years. Linda's income was all that kept our heads above water. But the poor economy paled in comparison to all else that 2009 had in store. It was that year that I lost two sons, a daughter, and a grandson.

Oh, no one died. There were no accidents, no heart attacks, no deadly diseases. All four are still around, and in good shape, in fact, thank God. But there are certain losses that are, in many ways, more difficult to take than death – those where a deliberate choice is made to hurt and destroy.

The first to go was Rob, a son-IN-LAW technically, but every bit a true son in my heart. Rob had proven himself in every way a good provider, a good husband to my daughter, and a great father to their children. I had grown to respect him and to love him as a son and as a dependable, trustworthy friend. As we sat at dinner eleven years earlier, and he asked my permission to marry Wendy, I tried to convey to him just how much trust he was asking for. He wanted me to give up the care of my first-born child and only daughter into his hands. He assured me that he understood that responsibility and was capable of the task, and worthy of the trust. He seemed he had been right, for all these years, until, in a single bad choice, he undermined all that we had built together. Another woman appeared to be the answer to all that was lacking in his life. She would be able to fill all the voids in his day. So, he left behind his wife, his children, me, and our entire family. Disappointment hit me like the water from a broken dam, washing away years of stability and comfort, and memories.

Everything in the process after that seemed calculated and mechanical from my limited point of view. There were financial arrangements to make, bill payments to split fairly, and children's schedules to be decided – all with emotions, seemingly set aside. He has no idea how angry I am, still, or hurt, for that matter. As to where the fault lies, no one can actually say.

No marriage is without its problems and there is always plenty of blame that can be shared. Linda and I are no exception. Problems, large and small, still arise from time to time, but we have been at it now for over 40 years. In all of those years it never once occurred to me to run when things got a little tough. It seems that every small problem we managed to work out along the way provided us with the tools, strength, and determination to tackle the larger ones that would surely come later. I do not think we have any special talent for making things work or the ability to miraculously smooth out the rough spots. We do have a commitment to one another that we refuse to compromise, and the example of parents who proved it could be done and done with grace and style.

I have never seen so much courage, strength, and determination in the face of disaster and devastation as I saw in my daughter through all of this. She truly became my greatest hero. There were those days when she had trouble finding a reason to go on – to even get out of bed. There were the days when the tears would not stop and the days when she questioned what she should have done differently; perhaps she had been the cause of all this. Her spirit was broken, but her soul was intact. I helped what little I could, but her real strength came when she looked to God for answers. Some answers never came - like how and why this should happen to her; but solutions to deal with it all did come. She worked through it – sometimes day by day, sometimes minute by minute. But that is who she is. She has an inner strength that even she was not aware of until she was forced to muster it to the surface. She is a survivor. She gives me hope that I, too, just might survive.

It was, in fact, Wendy who would recover much more quickly than I. She put her faith into practice. She managed, somehow, to find forgiveness in her heart for all the wrong that had been done, and now lives peaceably with her circumstances. I, on the other hand, have not yet achieved the same solitude. She asked me, just recently in the middle of one of my rants centered around some stupidity regarding her former husband, if I had "ever really forgiven anyone." Though it caught me off guard for a moment, I considered it, then answered, emphatically, "Yes I have, but I am not yet at a point to forgive him." She replied, "I know, but that is the only way to put it behind you. If you do not, the hurt will completely eat you alive."

I have thought about her question quite a bit since then. I have forgiven someone before, but maybe not to this magnitude. Maybe the things I offered forgiveness for were so small that they should not have affected me in the first place. Maybe I simply ignored the transgressions, not really forgiving them, because the people involved were not important enough to me for me to care. So, what does forgiveness really look like? Do I have to be friends with the person again? Am I supposed to act as though nothing ever happened? Do I have to make them part of my life again? How do I determine who actually deserves forgiveness? Should it even require earning, or is genuine forgiveness offered in the very face of injustice, not in sympathy for remorse? What is more, regardless of the need to forgive, I find trouble wanting to forgive. It would certainly be a lot easier to forgive following the proper punishment for all the wrongdoing, but the punishment never seems to come. Come to think of it, that is not real forgiveness either, just the satisfaction of a shallow, self-serving, I-told-you-so. Any consequences that I feel might be appropriate, if there are to be any, are not mine to determine anyway, nor mine to dole out. So, how do you forgive someone who has caused so much pain and damage; someone who lacks any semblance of remorse or responsibility for their actions, and who seems to have gotten away with it? The concept of true forgiveness is one that I have, obviously, yet to master.

I can certainly see the benefit of it – through Wendy. I think I know, down deep, the answers to most of my questions, especially in light of the forgiveness that has been offered me throughout my life – from family, from friends, and most of all, from God.

I certainly did not deserve it. I will keep working on it. The truth is, I do really miss Rob, and all the time we spent together. Maybe, someday....

Kevin, my biological son, was the next to go, taking with him his wife, Molly, and my grandson, Drew. Or it just may be that Molly was the one with the idea to "part company," taking Kevin and Drew - I can never be sure. I do know that tensions among the lot of us started just about the day Molly and Kevin met. The last three times that I have been to Kevin's home, he would not let me in the door. I made an unannounced visit to his office, hoping to catch him in, and try to resolve the issues between us – at least make a start. He was, in fact, there, and spotted me in the lobby in friendly conversation with the owner of his company. I caught a glimpse of the sneer on his face as he darted into a colleague's office, obviously avoiding me. As several of Kevin's other co-workers stopped to talk with me, Kevin took my brief distraction as an opportunity to duck out of the office where he was hiding and bolt down the hall to the back of the offices. I waited nearly an hour before leaving a note in his office, stating just how much I loved him, and wanted to solve our differences, asking him to give me a call. There was never a response.

Just a few months later, through a mutual friend, in a passing conversation, I got the shock of my life. He told me that Kevin had sold his house and had moved to Virginia – without a word, even a hint, that he was gone. I called, but my number has been blocked. I have written, but there has been no response. It is clear that he has erased all knowledge of me, his Mom, and our entire family, from his life.

It is now over nine years later, on a Sunday afternoon, and it is pouring rain. I cannot help but remember the day when Kevin was born.

It was pouring rain that day, as well. I had sat in the waiting area for quite some time, awaiting some news from the delivery room. Most of the family was there as well, as they had been for Wendy, except for Dad. He was working but had been notified that we were at the hospital, and he responded he would be on his way at the first chance he got. Oddly enough, Dad was the one person I wanted to see the most. The speculations, and horror stories being swapped by the remaining family had gotten on my last nerve. I was SO relieved when a nurse came out to tell us it would likely still be a while, and that everyone should take a break and get some lunch. That sounded like a good idea, and they all headed off to find something to eat. I opted to stay and have them bring something back for me to eat later.

It was something less than 15 minutes, I guess, when the elevator doors just in front of me opened, and off stepped Linda's doctor, pushing a cart with my beautiful baby boy. It sounds selfish, I know, but the timing could not have been more perfect – MY time, MY news, and MY son, with no one else around. I certainly wanted them all to share the joy, but, somehow, was glad to be the FIRST to meet this wonderful blessing. A very brief visit with doctor and son, assurance that all was well, and both were on the move again, headed to the hospital's nursery for more exams and preparation. I turned in my tracks, beaming from ear to ear, and the perfect timing continued. The elevator doors on the other side of the hall opened, and off stepped my Dad. I do not think I have ever been so glad to anyone in my life. I could not WAIT to tell him the news! He was the one person I needed near me the most at that moment. I broke into tears, and wrapped my arms around him, soaking wet raincoat, umbrella, hat, and all. His soaked clothing did not matter just then. Not surprisingly, he was every bit as excited as I was. Given the circumstances surrounding my own birth, and his experience, there was clearly a huge relief as well.*

All of this came back to mind, years later, following a phone call from Wendy. She said she had some news and was clearly upset about something. She began with the assurance that no one had died or gotten hurt – no one was sick. The news, she said, was about Kevin. It seems that there is some fluke with Facebook, on the internet, that randomly "pops up" some posting, or photo from some event or conversation, randomly, from someone you might have been in contact with, in the past. The information may be something familiar, or totally new – even postings that may have been blocked to you in times past. That was exactly the case when my great niece received a posting from Molly which she had shared with Wendy. It was a picture, and part of a conversation, between Molly and one of her friends - a Christmas family picture of Kevin, Molly, and the kids. THREE kids. It had been posted on January 11, 2019, with only one return comment to the friend included in the post. Molly's comment read "Chip turned 1 yesterday! If you can imagine, he is even sweeter than Paisley was at this age. And my Paisley is a funny, sassy, confident 4-year-old now! Drew is my steady, funny, imaginative 9-year-old now."

I have another grandson…..and he is a year old. Not only was my son not anxious to celebrate the news with me, he deliberately did not want me, or any other member of the family, to even know that Chip existed. The same had been true with Paisley. The contrast between my own feelings at the birth of my son, dying to share everything with my own father, and the thought that Kevin made every effort to make sure I knew nothing of the birth of his son, has left me confused, deflated, and totally devastated for days now. How can he possibly hate me that much? What could I have possibly done to him or his wife that would cause him to inflict that much pain on anyone?

There is a single Bible verse, found at Proverbs 22, verse six that has both given me hope and haunted me, for many years now. It reads "Train up a child in the way that he should go and when he is old, he will not depart from it." I find it encouraging, believing that no matter what happens, my son will return to the basics I tried to instill in him as he grew up. But, more recently, it has haunted me to think that maybe I failed to teach him enough or teach him correctly. He told me himself what a poor father he thought me to be and added that he and Molly had given serious consideration to not having children, faced with the prospect of having to introduce them to "people like you" (me). Though I have tried to accept his accusation as an outburst made in anger, with little thought behind it, and rely on the encouragement of those around me who tell me the same, there will always be that gnawing in the pit of my stomach that makes me wonder if there was not certainly something that I could have done differently – something that I could have done better. The consequences may very well be that I never get the opportunity to know some of my own grandchildren. I am truly grateful to God for yet another beautiful, healthy, grandson, but I do not know how I can bear living out the rest of my life without ever even meeting him.

Mom had been in labor with me for 27 hours. In 1952, performing a C-section was never given any consideration, short of a last resort. Medical techniques had not developed to the point where it was actually safe to deliver a baby in that manner, let alone commonplace. Mom's doctor – our family GP – finally came out to describe the circumstance in detail. He said they had decided to "take" the baby – me – using forceps. He further added that he may have to deliver me "in pieces", actually asking Dad to decide, should the option present itself, which one of us – me or Mom - should be saved. My aunt described me as "the ugliest baby she had ever seen", red and bruised, with forceps marks all over my face. I survived. Mom survived. Even Dad survived. Thank you, Dr. Albert Morris, for using all the skill you had to make that happen. Thank you, God, for the plans you had for all of us that even Dr. Morris could not foresee.

twenty

I took Mom & Dad to church today. Not a big deal; at least not to anyone else. But for me, it was a big deal – a really big deal. Mom cannot drive right now. At 87 years old, she and Dad are normally as independent as anyone. She cooks every day, keeps house, still sews, and makes quilts. They go out with friends and, usually, she drives just about anywhere they need to go. Dad has long since given up driving. His eyesight is nearly gone – macular degeneration – and his hearing, even with his hearing aids, is none too good. But Mom has been having a few random bouts with dizziness – nearly passing out at times. I convinced her (made the appointment myself) to see her doctor, who advised her not to drive for a while until he could find the problem. They skipped church on the first Sunday, but staying home, especially from church is simply not an option for those two. They are faithful to a fault, and, even more, they really enjoy being there for worship. They never miss, if they can help it. If they were the only ones in attendance, they would probably still go.

Mom hates to impose . . . never wants to cause any trouble

or inconvenience for anyone, even when it really is no bother at all. She is that much like her own mother, who often would not let you help her no matter how inconvenient that actually became. But this was "church." Arrangements of some sort must be made. Several neighbors offered to take her, but finally, she broke down and accepted my offer to drive them myself. They had arranged lunch with Mom's sister, who would take them home afterward. Mom would pay for lunch, of course. We arrived with their usual half-an-hour-early promptness. I dropped them off at the front door and returned to my own church for services there. No big deal. Boringly uneventful. That is, to everyone except me

You see, my Mom and Dad will never fully understand what it means to me to be able to help them in even the smallest ways. True, they cared for my grandmother for years – furnished her a place to live, all of her transportation and meals, paid all of her bills, and looked after her day and night until her death. They remember how much work it was now, as they look to me for the slightest assistance, but have forgotten just how much they wanted to care for her. They did not really feel the obligation nearly as much as the desire. I watched them sacrifice their own lives for hers without a second thought or complaint – or a "thank you" from siblings who remained conveniently distant or otherwise occupied. Mine is no mere obligation either. It was this church where they had carried me – from the day I was born; long before I was able to go on my own, or even choose to go at all. It was here that I learned the value of friends, integrity, responsibility, and the importance of worship. It was this church, and these people who showed me the power of prayer and that the impossible is, in fact, possible through God. It was here that I met God for myself. My own children were born into this church family as well and were cared for just as I had been. I totally get what this church means to them because it holds the same memories and importance for me

But this is about more than just where I took them. I am certainly hopeful that Mom will be released to drive again within the next week or so. Maybe not. It crossed my mind that this might just be the next phase of care that they need. I look back over the past several years at just how we have all arrived at the arrangements now in place and am amazed at what has taken place. When I began the cabinet business that I am in, my average week involved four or five jobs with a very small price tag each. As doctor's visits became more numerous and chores around Mom's and Dad's house became more demanding, my jobs dwindled to around half the original number, but the average value easily doubled. I had more time to devote to the growing needs that my parents were no longer able to fulfill for themselves, with an equal reduction in workload, without a reduction in income. Recently, doctor's visits, trips to the drug store, grocery store or bank, or some other event requiring my presence, have become almost daily. Strangely enough, my business has dropped, yet again, to nearly half the previous number of jobs, and, again, nearly doubled in average value. My schedule is now more flexible than ever before.

Coincidence? I think not. I choose to believe, instead, that God not only controls my life but takes an active part in my daily routine. He knows how much I want to attend to the details of my parents' life, just as He knows how much they need my help. The rest – the schedules and routines – He orchestrates. I could never have devised such a plan on my own and brought it to life. But He could. He has. He has allowed me the absolute honor of doing all the things that make life a little simpler, a little better, and a little easier for the parents who invested so much in me and has allowed me to do it without the inconvenience or sacrifice that they had to make. How could I not believe in a God who cares for me – and them; a God who takes an active role in my life; a God whose plan is beyond comprehension? How could anyone not believe?

twenty-one

Luke 12:40 says "Be ye therefore ready also: for the Son of Man cometh at an hour when ye think not." That hour came for my father on the morning of February 22, 2014. He awoke to a routine call of nature and his stirring had awakened Mom. On his return to bed, she asked if he was alright. It was obvious to her that he was not feeling himself and went to the bathroom for a cool, wet washcloth. Mom had always been convinced that a cool cloth was a sure way to improve a person's health, no matter the ailment. She wiped his face and asked again if he was okay. He replied, simply, "Not really. I feel like I might be about to die." With that, he lay back down in bed and closed his eyes. His breathing slowed, his heart stopped, and he released his last breath. With the silence of that last breath, he left us.

Though a tragedy for us, Dad finally found the relief he had wanted for some time. His hearing and eyesight had failed. His appetite was gone. Days passed without purpose, and he often lost track of day and night. His cane just barely got him around the house and the task of dressing himself had become nearly an hour-long chore. Even though Dad was not truly anxious to leave this world – to leave Mom – it seemed sometimes as though he knew his time approached.

On his last cardiologist's visit, his doctor informed us that he would be closing the office where we usually saw him and would be relocating quite some distance away. Dad replied simply that the relocation would not be a problem for him, and commented to me later that we probably did not need to plan on seeing the doctor again. I insisted that the distance was nothing to worry about and that I would be glad to continue driving him wherever necessary, but it was not the distance that was on his mind. "Well, we'll see," he said. He never made the next visit. I will always be grateful to God for the calm and the peace that surrounded Dad's death and could ask for no more when the end of my own life draws near.

It must be said of Dad, that, above all, he was a man who had his priorities in order. Though circumstances would sometimes intervene, he always managed to keep first things first. His job, and even more so, his customers were certainly a priority to him. Family – even more important, especially Mom and myself. Nothing, much, would keep him out of church, every time an opportunity presented itself, but above all – God and his relationship with God – took first place, no matter what. It took me many years to separate my own relationship with my church from that with the Lord, but it was exemplified in my father. He had a clear understanding of the difference and never equated the two. A simple confrontation with the church pushed him to prove his allegiance.

I must have been somewhere around seven years old or so, approaching summer break from school. While traveling around the state, Dad had begun to see signs at a number of churches advertising "Vacation Bible School" – a one or two-week bible study camp for kids featuring music, arts & crafts, and recreation. Our church had never held such an event, but Dad became convinced that we should. He knew that it was God's conviction, not just a whim on his part – he knew nothing about even how to begin. Dad served as a deacon at our church and had, for as long as I had been around. At the very next meeting, he shared his idea with the pastor and other deacons. He could almost hear them all laughing at the idea – even the pastor

– a man of true faith in what could happen when the impossible was placed in the hands of God. But even he refused to budge, arguing that no one knew how to organize a Vacation Bible School, there would not be enough workers, and, most importantly, there were no more than a dozen children in our entire church that were school age. The idea was completely absurd. Dad's discouragement was obvious, to say the least, and his aggravation lingered over the next couple of weeks. He just could not let go of what, he was certain, God had placed in his mind and on his heart.

It was less than a week until school would be out for the Summer and approaching the ideal time to schedule VBS. Dad was just getting up from the breakfast table on Saturday morning. Taking the last of his coffee with him, he walked to the dining room window and was looking out over the front lawn. A car was turning into our driveway, coasting the last few feet, powered now, only by its own inertia rather than the engine. A young man stepped out, walked around to the front of the car, opened the hood, and began staring blankly into the engine compartment. After a long consideration of his options, the young man closed the hood and began walking toward the house, in a despondent gate. Dad finished off the last drop of coffee, dropped off his cup at the sink, and headed out to see how he might help. The visitor forced a smile and introduced himself, as he explained that his car, (recently offering decreased cooperation), was now officially dead.

Rather than asking for help, he asked if Dad knew where he might find work, at least temporarily, that would afford him the chance to have repairs made. Dad explained that this was a rural, farm community, where few, if any, jobs were ever available. He then asked where the young man was from, and what kind of work he was looking for. He said he was a college student from the northern part of the country and was willing to do ANYTHING to earn a few dollars. Dad persisted with his question, asking what had brought him this far south, and what kind of work he was capable of.

His answer should not have surprised us, I guess, but certainly set us back on our heels. "I am working on my college degree in seminary, hoping to eventually be a youth minister," he replied. "I am traveling around the country for the summer, visiting various churches in an attempt to organize Vacation Bible Schools wherever I can."

No one laughed this time. This minister-to-be became our guest for the next few weeks as Dad offered him our garage/rental house for as long as needed. Several men of the church with auto repair skills pitched in to fix the disgruntled automobile - absolutely afraid NOT to - and at no cost to our God-sent newcomer. To this day, I could not tell you where the 125 kids came from as we opened VBS for the first time, but I can assure you that there was never a question about the event for the next year or any year thereafter. God had spoken, and was able to impact hundreds of people, all because my father listened, and was faithful to keep God, not the church or his pastor as his first priority.

Linda and I stayed with Mom at night for about a week and a half following Dad's death. She finally insisted that she would be okay, and for us to return home, but her insistence was clearly an attempt to convince herself more than us. We eventually did, seeing her every day, calling before bedtime, and having her call me each morning. We made sure that she had proper meals, insisting that she eat out with us as often as possible, especially after all the food brought in by neighbors and family had diminished. She was determined to live on her own and not to "bother" anyone with having to care for her. I supported her effort, telling her that there was no reason she should not give it a try if that's what she wanted. I knew, however, that at some point there would come the need for a closer watch on her health and daily activities. I tried to drive her wherever she wanted to go, but that need for independence compelled her to make the weekly trips to the hairdresser, a stop-off by the grocery store, and a do-not-miss trip to church – Wednesday and Sunday – on her own.

I have always had a pretty good idea for design and have never been afraid to make a huge mess of a perfectly good house, attempting to make it a little better. I had tried for years to figure out a way to incorporate a bedroom into the main level of our home (two-story with three bedrooms upstairs) but had never found the right formula to make it work. The house was still the same, but, I guess, my perspective and motivation had changed.

There was a room on the main level that started life as a sunroom. It transformed over the years into a breakfast room, sewing room, and now, a conglomeration of sewing room, TV room, and my office – not pretty, but workable. As though it was originally meant to be, I envisioned a design for a bedroom, full bath, and walk-in closet, all fitted neatly within the space of my ill-purposed menagerie, with a little help from the adjoining dining room. My office would fit efficiently in the corner of the family room. I began work, without telling Mom. She would certainly rebel at the idea of moving in with us – an inconvenience, a waste of money – she was staying put! About halfway through construction, I brought her over to check out my latest "project," making it clear that it was something Linda and I had always wanted to do. Her first question upon entering the house was "Is this going to be my room?" I was taken back a little at her response, but still a little skeptical as to where this might be headed. I explained that it could be hers – maybe for an overnight visit occasionally or even a weekend now and then. She could come when she wanted, if she wanted, and return home on her own schedule, and it would serve as a good spot for the grandkids when they come to visit. She felt like that was an adequate plan for the room, but insisted that she would live alone, in her own house, as long as she was able.

Then, over the next couple of days, she began calling everyone she knew, bragging about the beautiful bedroom and bath that I had built, just for her. None of us had any way of knowing the events to come during the next weeks, but just perhaps, Mom had somewhat the same kind of insight into the future that Dad had surrounding his last doctor's visit.

Mom had suffered for several months with leg and knee pain, sometimes to the point that she was unable to walk. Several doctors had prodded, poked, injected, and medicated the problem with little success, all chalking up the problem to arthritis and old age. A friend at church told her of the success they had with a particular doctor and suggested that she give him a try. I looked him up for her, only to find that he was a partner in the group of doctors she had been seeing all along. She insisted on giving him a try anyway. To the surprise of us both, an x-ray indicated an obvious torn meniscus and debris around the kneecap to be the culprit. I was even more surprised when he recommended surgery to make the repair. Really? Surgery? At 90 years old? Are you sure?

The surgery actually went very well – in by 8:00 and out by 3:00 and up and walking that afternoon. Almost apologetically, Mom said that she might have to spend a night or two with us in her new bedroom, just until the soreness went away. Now when you are twenty, even 30 years old, recovery from meniscus surgery is tough, but with a little downtime and a little exercise, you are back going again. But not at 90. She did show some improvement every day, but the pace was much slower than she ever imagined, and that was frustrating for her. I know, too, that without Dad by her side, the task of getting well was even more daunting. But she tried, and exercised, and followed her doctor's every instruction – and got better. She seemed quite comfortable staying at our house with the 'night or two' now stretching into the sixth week. By now she had transferred most of her clothes and personal effects to her temporary home. Though she continued to talk of returning home, she often allowed herself to entertain the idea that she now needed more help, for simpler tasks, than in the recent past. She missed her ability to drive her car most of all. Driving seemed to be her embodiment of independence, and that was gone – at least for now.

First in a wheelchair, then a walker, and finally with just the aid of a cane, she regained her mobility for the most part. At her doctor's instruction, she had begun a therapy regimen two days each week. I drove her there, and to her weekly hairdressing appointment, and even to church when she felt like going. She would often attend church on Sunday, then have lunch and spend the afternoon with her sister. Her walking improved, but the void left by my father's death grew deeper by the day. I continued to offer a supporting hand, mostly for my own peace of mind, hoping to avoid a fall but found I could offer little else to console her loss.

Linda and I had just begun a fairly substantial renovation on the house at the lake (again), stealing a day or two at the time to get things organized. Mom even went with us several times, facing yet another bank of memories that reflected the shadow of her husband. On one weekend near mid-September, we made plans for another trip to the house and asked Mom if she would like to go. After some thought, she decided that she would rather spend a little more time with her sister and insisted that we go without her. She was walking well and there was a definite anticipation about plans the two of them had made for the weekend. We decided to go, dropping off Mom at her sister's home on the way.

Just twenty-four hours later, on Saturday morning, I answered my phone to hear news of the one thing we had all tried so hard to avoid – Mom had fallen, while getting out of the car, and was in the hospital with a broken hip. If there was any good in this whole event it was that Mom had very little pain, especially given the nature of her injury. The following morning, during a very brief and simple surgery, doctors were able to insert a steel rod into the bone in her leg and secure the break with screws. A full recovery was expected. Just having gotten back on her feet from the knee repair, Mom now faced the prospect of starting the process of healing all over again. Monday and Tuesday were met with improvements each day and still only a minimum of pain. Efforts were made to find a short-term rehab facility before returning home. Surprising improvements continued on every front. Late on Tuesday afternoon, Mom was drifting in and out of a light sleep. At one point, she seemed to awaken briefly and called Dad's name. Linda walked to her bedside and touched her on the arm, asking if she was alright. She said she was fine. As I approached her bedside, she apologetically added "You are going to have to take care of things." I assured her that I would handle whatever came up – with the details of her rehab, her return home, and her recovery circulating through my mind - as she drifted back off to sleep, rousing periodically to continue her conversation with Dad. Later that evening, I said goodnight and promised to see her first thing in the morning. I headed home, with Linda close behind, and without any clue of what "things" I would have to handle.

The next phone call came just a few hours later, at 3:30 a.m. on Wednesday morning. A doctor on the other end said that Mom had taken a turn for the worse. The nurses had checked her at 3:00 and found her vital signs all near perfect. She said she had no pain and wanted no pain medicine. Now, just 30 minutes later, the same nurses were not able to get any response – no heartbeat, no breathing, no response of any kind. The doctor described a team of workers now surrounding my Mom, offering whatever emergency measures they could, in rotation, but without any sign of success. She described their aggressive efforts, and then asked, "Do you want us to continue? What should we do next?" There was only one reasonable answer. I told them to stop.

I have no doubt that many may find this idea a real stretch, but I have not been able to get Tuesday afternoon out of my mind. Mom and Dad always made major decisions together. They always supported one another's wishes, but talked things out, just to allow the other's point of view to shed a different light on the situation. I believe with all of my heart that, when Mom called Dad's name that afternoon, it was in the middle of a conversation with him about what was to come next. She was ready to leave, but needed his approval, and he agreed that it was time. The look about her when we arrived at the hospital so early Wednesday morning told me that their decision was a good one. Just like Dad, she left this world silently, without pain, without fear, ready to go, and fully prepared for the next life. I would not trade the opportunity to care for her, in my home, for the last six weeks of her life for anything. It was truly an honor to have such an opportunity.

Time of death was officially set at 4:00 am. I am quite sure that the doctor was just a little off though, because, as we returned home, I happened to notice that the grandfather clock just outside Mom's bedroom door had stopped running at 3:47.

twenty-two

Throughout my life, my Mom often reminded me to be cautious of just how much importance I placed on myself in whatever role I played. She encouraged self-worth, certainly, but warned against reaching the point where a person feels that they could never be replaced. She would say, "If you really want to know what you are worth, stick your finger into a bucket of water, then pull it out, and see how big a hole you leave." That has remained a constant reminder to me that no one person, least of all me, serves as the center of the universe. No one is so important that they cannot be replaced. Along a similar vein, I was reminded recently that no one person is exempt from the pitfalls and ailments that this life often brings.

Once I turned 60 years old, Dr. Anders, my primary physician, began to include a PSA test – Prostate Specific Antigen test – among the other standards in my routine blood work. It is designed as an early detection indicator of prostate cancer. According to David, the test should produce a relative score of less than "4". My first test came in at 2.7. One year later, my score jumped to 4.4, and prompted a referral to a Urologist.

Following a brief exam, and the explanation that this particular test carried only about a 30% accuracy rate, he discounted the incident as nothing of concern. One more year behind me and the test returned at 4.5 – virtually unchanged. My fourth, and most recent, test prompted the most concern at a score of 5.3, and a return trip to Dr. Duralde. As he entered the room, I greeted him with "Hello doctor," to which he responded "Well, your luck has finally run out." That is never a line you want to hear from any doctor, I can assure you. He proceeded to explain that, although he was not concerned so much with how high the number was itself, he was seriously concerned with the direction that the numbers were headed, and said it was time to take the "next step" – yet another ominous term. "Believe it or not," he explained, "the next step is actually a biopsy." My mind now began to conjure images of hospital gowns, needles, surgery, and all things not so much fun. I pushed him toward some possible alternate explanations for the increased numbers – something other than cancer, but to no avail. Acknowledging the outside possibility of some other cause, he would not budge from the need for further testing. I consented and began to shift my thoughts away from the upcoming procedure and a little more toward various types of treatment, in the event of.... The following week, the surgical office called to set an appointment – only available on Fridays. The next available slot was two weeks away, 9:00 a.m. So it was set.

Linda reminded me later, as I reviewed my entire day with her, that the particular Friday that I had selected was actually the one just prior to the Memorial Day weekend, and we were scheduled to be at the lake with her whole family. I returned to my calendar and realized another advantage of pushing this procedure back a week. On the next Thursday, June 1st, I would begin my eligibility for Medicare, and my supplemental insurance, as I would turn 65 years old in the middle of that month. Now the entire ordeal was three weeks away. If I could have somehow gone through the testing that very same day, and had the results back within the hour, I would have readily done so. Waiting is terrible – on your mind, your nerves, your diet, your sleep – it occupies your every thought while your mind conjures possibilities that range far outside reality. I tried to stick with the facts and wait it out.

I will spare the details of exactly how the test was carried out but suffice it to say that Dr. Duralde removed six samples of actual prostate tissue using a hollow, spring-loaded, biopsy needle, following several injections to deaden the area. Those injections would later prove to be fairly effective over four of the samples he removed, leaving the remaining two quite memorable, to say the least. The entire procedure took about 15 minutes, and I was back at home within 45 minutes of having left for the appointment. Home again, to wait again. Results would not be back for yet another week. Relieved, certainly, that the biopsy was at least behind me, my mind once again began its creative search for possible outcomes.

The call came earlier than expected, on Wednesday afternoon – the results were back, and the doctor would like to see me for a follow up visit on Friday. I am sure the nurse could hear the begging in my voice as I asked if there was no sooner time to come – maybe even later that day. She finally consented to work me in on Thursday afternoon – 4:00. Linda went with me, and we sat as every single patient in the waiting room was called, leaving only the two of us, as closing time for the office approached. As I was sure my turn must be only moments away, another patient came in – an emergency case that would occupy the next half hour. Would the waiting never end? Not that I was so anxious to find out bad news, but no news is nearly unbearable. Called into the exam room, finally, and yet another 15 minutes of frazzled nerves, Dr. Duralde finally appeared. He began to apologize for the delay, and briefly explain the emergency that had occurred, when he must have seen how totally rattled I was – literally shaking, I am sure – and abruptly interrupted his explanation of the delay.

The slightest beginning of a smile, creeping from the corners of his mouth, was all I really needed. "I should have just called you," he said. "You are perfectly fine. All of your tests came back negative." Life was good. I felt myself breathe again. He went on to explain to Linda that a PSA blood test has been found to be only about 30% accurate but remains the only test available to detect the early stages of prostate cancer. It is therefore necessary to take the test regularly, at my age, and pay attention to the changes in the results.

So, after all that, nothing really came out of the entire ordeal. All of the worry, even the testing was for nothing. Not quite. I did learn that, despite the elevated test scores, I do NOT have cancer. I was reminded, too, of just how good the God that I serve really is. I find myself so very blessed, in so many areas, that I fear I often consider those blessings to be the norm for me – expected and leaving me immune from those things suffered by friends and family around me. I was reminded that life, mine included, is a fragile gift that should never be taken for granted. I saw, once again, the life that God has given me, and found myself humbled and undeserving of all that I have and enjoy. I do not feel that I "dodged a bullet" or "got lucky this time" as is often our resolve. In fact, I do not believe in "luck" of any sort – good or bad. I believe only in divine providence. Thank you, Lord. I think I may need to keep a bucket of water handy, just to stick my finger in now and then.

Throughout my years in school, and far beyond, I have heard the alliteration of life as compared to the seasons of the year. It seems that there was always more emphasis on the "Fall" and "Winter" of a person's life – the later years, as we grow older – than on the earlier seasons. As I have begun to add a few more years myself, I have come to realize that there are indeed far more seasons to life than just those four associated with the changes in weather. At some point in our lives, nearly all of us face seasons of prosperity, seasons of depravity, seasons of health, or illness, growth and expansion, or cutbacks and loss. There are seasons of depression and seasons of optimism. I am talking about those times that span more than just a few days or weeks, beyond just one project or effort, and, though without a specific timeframe, last long enough to have a significant impact on the history of our lives. These "seasons" are not just one blip on the radar, but must be worked through, dealt with, sorted out, survived, and, hopefully, learned from.

The problem with life seasons comes in actually knowing what season you are in at any given time. It is easy to identify Spring by the sight of new growth; budding flowers, sprouting leaves, and green grass clearly tell us what time of year we are in. Likewise, the colors of Fall or the chilly temperatures of Winter leave no doubt as to the exact time of the year. But as events, surroundings, and circumstances in our life give way to new experiences, there is no way to envision what is around the corner, how long it might last, or how intensely it will affect us long term. We are given no warning as to the effort it will take to survive or the rewards that lie ahead for the taking.

Even in the middle of some life "season" we often have no clue as to its identity, until it is over. Only over a long span of time are we able to look back and see just how high we actually soared, or just how low the valley and how rugged the terrain we have traveled. That has to be by design. Were we given forewarning of what was to come, we would most certainly opt to forego the pain, and in the process, lose out on some of life's greatest treasures. It is through trials that we find strength, and through survival that we gain perseverance. Success and reward grow opportunity and responsibility. All are interlinked and each is vital to the "year" of our lives.

We all spend a great deal of time planning for the later years in our life – economically, physically, - and even making preparations to care for those who are likely to survive us. We plan for the larger obstacles and opportunities, but rarely give much thought to the details. Those are left to those who become responsible for our day-to-day care. To that end, I would like to make a "wish list" for myself, to give to my children, should God choose to allow me to last beyond my capacity to tend to the finer points of my own care.

For my children:

See to it that I get all the medicine that I truly need but spare me multiple doses of "let's try this", or "this might help" that are often doled out in an attempt to compensate for age, not disease.

Do not consider me properly dressed with food stains on my clothes, my pants unzipped, my shirttail only half tucked, pants and shirt that obviously do not match, or my hair (if any remains) uncombed.

Do not let me sit at the table with food on my face without telling me or removing it.

In short . . . help me to maintain at least some semblance of dignity.

Further,

Be brutally honest with me – regarding my health, my care, my finances, and about my attitude and behavior. Do not allow me to get away with being rude or abusive to anyone.

Talk to me, not about me, for as long as I am able to understand.

Allow me to try those things that I think I can do, so long as I do no harm to myself or inconvenience others.

Tie my shoes without my having to ask when I no longer can.

Should you ever make the choice that I live with you (and it is your choice), make sure that is what is best for me and for you. Noble intentions, though greatly appreciated, do not qualify anyone for the type of care that might be necessary. The simple knowledge that you put your life on hold to accommodate mine will just make mine worse. I have joked for years with Wendy that I dare not cross her very often since she will be the one who chooses my nursing home eventually. Assisted living facilities, retirement homes, nursing homes – whatever they might be called by then – should not be a last resort, and, in fact, might offer a welcome change of pace for everyone involved, including me. Consider them as a viable and even welcome alternative, providing not only a professional level of assistance but the companionship of others like me, and do so while I am still in a frame of mind to discuss it with you.

Finally,

Do not be afraid to touch me, even hug me, just because I am old, wrinkled, and fragile.

As I have grown older, I have come to believe that the human touch is one of the most powerful tools at our disposal. It can say much more than words ever could. A touch can indicate love or intimacy, but it can just as readily offer support, sympathy, understanding, and friendship. It signifies trust and comfort. A touch might come from our closest love or a total stranger – but either can transfer enormous power and is felt clearly into our soul. Its absence for any significant period of time can literally draw all the life from a waiting soul.

There is just one more thing. If God should decide to take me, suddenly, by any means, just a little earlier than you might have imagined, and in otherwise good health, do not be sad for me. In fact, be grateful that He blessed me with the opportunity to bypass the endless schedule of doctors' visits – their pokes and prodding, - the pills, the shots, and the side effects they produce, and the routine hospital stays that seem to come one on the heels of another, and especially the long days and seemingly endless nights with little or nothing to do, and without the strength to even want to. I, certainly, could find no disappointment in an early departure from such a dismal existence. And when I am gone – do not feel guilty at the relief you feel from no longer having to care for me. It is a heavy burden to bear that responsibility. Feel glad to finally be relieved of it. You have earned the rest. Likewise, there should be no shame in enjoying anything monetary that I manage to leave behind. If there is anything left, it is there, intended for your use and benefit. It is my last gift to you, hoping to make your life a tiny bit easier or more enjoyable. Do with any of it as you please. Memories are great, but stuff just takes up space, and fills your attic and basement. Keep what you really want to use and turn the rest into something good for you or others.

twenty-three

I am a firm believer that, at least every now and then, you should have dessert first. Not always, necessarily, but at least, every now and then. It is not as easy as you think. On numerous occasions, I have instructed a waitress that I would START with a particular dessert, FOLLOWED by my main meal. Nine times out of ten, the meal comes first – no dessert. She certainly heard what I said. She just did not take me seriously. NOBODY has dessert first. And just why not? Why must I be forced to eat things in a predetermined order and must wait for what I want most? Life is just too short to wait until the end of the meal for the good stuff.

I feel like I spend all too much of my life waiting. I wait for my wife to come home from work or for her to get ready to go out, wait at the doctor's office for the appointment scheduled for at least 45 minutes ago, wait for the bank to open, wait for a customer to make a decision, wait for a check to arrive…. but I have realized that I also wait for things on a much larger scale, as well. It is not the few extra minutes here or there…even a day or so now and then that eats up our lives. Sure, those minutes add up to days, weeks, and even years, over a lifetime. Even so, I have to believe that the most common regret at the end of even the greatest life, is that of waiting just a little too long – on something – and missing it entirely. I have come to the conclusion that pure practicality will smother the most ambitious of souls if allowed the opportunity.

Certainly, there is a place for practicality. I know several people who lack any comprehension of the concept. Their lives lack any stability or direction, and they seem to drift through life without purpose or plans for the future. They are pretty much useless to themselves and the world around them. None of them are happy. But practical thinking does not have to dominate our lives, either. It should serve more as a guideline – a rule of thumb. Linda and I decided to delay having children until "we could afford it."

We soon discovered that we were on the road to NEVER having children. Instead, we decided to figure out how to make it work, as best we knew how and got started with our family. We had put off buying a house for the same reason. When we finally did sign on the dotted line for our first home, the notion of actually paying the daunting $267.00 mortgage note each month was overwhelming. But we survived – the house payment and our first child. The world did not end. And with those triumphs came the courage to tackle bigger challenges. There would be larger homes with bigger house notes, new jobs in unfamiliar surroundings, a different church, new schools, new friends, and even a second child. Life got better every time we ventured outside the very familiar and the very comfortable. We did so cautiously – perhaps too cautiously – but we ventured, nonetheless. Timing is never right. Waiting for the right TIME to do something is a poor excuse for fear. On that point, reason seems to contradict itself.

Several times over the past thirty or so years, I have come to the very practical, well-thought-out conclusion, that Linda and I should sell our home and move someplace else. The house was in great condition, and at the top of its market. It had served us well, but we both would enjoy a change. What is more, over the next few years, we would certainly be facing some significant repair expenses, as with any home. Everything pointed to the logical thinking conclusion that we should move…but it just did not seem like the right TIME. So, we stayed – for well over thirty years now – through three major renovations. We still look around sometimes, at more "house" than we could ever need, and comment at what we would like to do differently, should we ever decide to build again, just waiting for the right time. But the RIGHT TIME just is not right – now. What's more, I have recently noticed that "it" has started. I can feel it and "it" may only prolong the waiting.

Defining "it" is quite impossible. There are symptoms, but not a defined prognosis. It is related to age, certainly, but "it" does not start at a specific age or time. "It" does not punch a clock or follow a calendar. Health is a factor too, as is attitude, patience, and ambition. Everyone is subject to the symptoms – some more severely than others, yet no one wakes up one morning to the sudden realization that they have them. There are no pills available, nor any cure. They sneak up on you, slowly, and take over, silently. Phrases are often tossed around to identify this phenomenon, like "reaching that point in time," or, maybe, "that season in life."

The whole process is littered with aggravation. In my case, it started with reading glasses, and an unrelenting ego that would not let me be seen using them – at least until the inconveniences that come with not being able to see, outweighed the giggles from those around me who will – all too shortly – be reaching for their own pair. Then, no sooner did I get used to pulling out those annoying, half-framed nose-pinchers before looking through the junk mail, than I was confronted with an envelope in the mail containing an invitation from AARP to become a member! In oversized print, no less. Of all the nerve!! "Senior citizen" discounts now come without inquiring as to my age, from children behind the register who must certainly have not finished middle school yet. Finally, as if AARP ads were not enough, I now receive regular publications about estate planning and burial arrangements!

And where did all of those pesky aches and pains come from? I haven't done anything that I don't normally do. At least, things I used to be able to do. My doctor tells me they are common "at my age." I nearly decked him. I can still hold my own when it comes to hard work, and my calendar is still full, but the pace has slowed a little – and I usually pay for it a couple of days later. Speaking of calendars, I am finding it most helpful to write everything down and not commit it to memory. I have always had an excellent memory, but I guess there is just so MUCH that I have to remember these days that some of the details tend to slip through the cracks. Dates, appointments, people's names, directions, a to-do list – all those are probably best accounted for with a note somewhere if I can just remember where I write it down. But the biggest aggravation has got to be people. Stupidity is rampant and there is no cure for that either. Fast food restaurants top the list of left-my-brain-at-home employees – incapable of taking a three-item order and getting it right, even when repeated four times - but it certainly does not stop there. I get almost all of my customers through referrals, and I am convinced that, recently, my name and phone number must have circulated, somehow, through every mental ward in the state. The list of ridiculous questions and demands seems endless. I truly believe that completion of a course in common sense should be mandatory to graduate from any learning institution and tested before hiring someone to even the most menial of tasks. It has become a rare commodity.

twenty-four

I have become a creature of habit and find myself often annoyed by the details of life – especially when someone changes one of them. Why can't the little things just be left alone? Was it absolutely necessary to move the trash can at Chick-fil-A so near the door – right in the flow of traffic - and shrink it to half its former size? Why would anyone really need to put the napkins on one end of the lobby and the plastic forks on the other end … and then mix the forks and spoons in the same bin? While I am at it, who is the genius at Lowes who decided to put light fixtures on one aisle near the electrical supplies, while the light bulbs are housed four isles over? Tools are ALL located together in "tool world" except painting tools – located in the paint department, and drywall tools – located near roofing, of course! My patience grows thin. I just may not go back there again. I am beginning to suspect that "it" may have begun invading my patience, as well.

What scares me the most is that I am learning to cope – to actually get used to all of the invasion into my normalcy. I now have several pairs of reading glasses, conveniently littered around those places where they are most frequently needed. My clipboard now carries my notes, along with a concise to-do list and calendar, along with my checkbook, pens, and paper. I have adjusted to scheduling just a little less to do each day and gladly accept any and all help that might be offered. The pain of AARP membership has been tempered, slightly, by an occasional discount offered around town (though the membership card is still stored in the BACK of my wallet, out of sight). I suppose I do have a definition for "it," truth be known – I am simply growing older.

But I REFUSE to give in to age. It will slow me down, most certainly. It will alter my schedule, my pace, and my capacity. I can learn to adjust to that – maybe even enjoy it, in some cases. I will continue to struggle with senseless changes in details, and the brainless drones flooding the retail industry, and the fast-food business, and I will NEVER grow accustomed to just plain STUPIDITY. But I will constantly seek the single thing that I am certain is the key to longevity, and that is relevance. During a conversation, recently, with my daughter and granddaughter, in a discussion of what my granddaughter wanted to pursue as a career, I capped off the conversation with a very philosophical quip, especially for me, instructing her – however, she chose to make a living - to follow her passion.

It was at that point that my 9-year-old grandson asked a question that caught me a little off guard: "What is your passion?" he asked. It took me a minute or two to answer. I truly believed what I had just told my granddaughter to be true, but I wonder if I had ever stopped to consciously think about what it is that satisfies me the most. I realized quickly that my passion was not the daily routine of what I do, but rather the framework – the core – of why I do what I do. I have worked in the building component business. I have built and remodeled houses and commercial buildings. I currently work in the cabinet and countertop business.

In quickly scanning over what I had done, what I liked to do, and what I was good at, I realized that the common thread was, and always had been – design. My passion was in design work – whether it was a set of roof trusses, a new house or basement makeover, my own home or lake house, or someone's new kitchen.

I am actually able to fulfill my passion by any number of functions, so long as the core reason is in play. That flexibility has allowed me to change jobs, even shift careers, a number of times over the years and easily settle back into a comfort zone. My passion was still the center of focus. Through my passion, I have been able to find relevance.

I plan to retire - soon now, I hope - but I never planned to quit. I may leave the daily grind of the workforce, but as long as I can be useful, even in the smallest capacity, to myself, and, hopefully, those around me, I can survive. It is the relevance that pushes us into tomorrow, preserves our health, and satisfies us. When we lose that, we die. But that death does not come suddenly. Life is diverse, and we often find significance – in varying degrees – in more than one place. A job, a church, a neighborhood, friends, and family can all offer opportunities to make ourselves useful, even well into late life. When any one area finds us no longer necessary, we are afforded an opportunity to give up, and, if we choose to do so, a part of us dies. I have attempted to serve, for a number of years, on the technical team at my church. I am proud to have actually implemented a good percentage of the processes and functions still in use.

Design, as it turns out, plays a key role in what I do there as well. But the position has grown far past me, and I am no longer a necessary part of the process. Others now have taken on the tasks that I used to perform, and have changed them - adapted them to suit themselves. I am no longer needed. No sour grapes here, though. Understand, the job now NEEDS a younger mind – sharper, quicker, with more enthusiasm than I now possess. It requires new ideas to keep up with changing technology and a faster pace. I get that. And I can accept that. I can choose to quit – and die a little at the loss – or continue to do what I can, and find other opportunities, in addition, to remain viable. I choose to live outside my previous role on the team.

In another area, however, beyond my control, my son has made it clear that, where I was once a vital source of advice, assistance, inspiration, and friendship in his life, I am no longer necessary. That portion of my life, for now, has died.

a random thought . . .

This has been an up-and-down week. The highs were really up there, and the lows – hard to bear. I have had Kevin, Molly, and their kids on my mind much more than usual for some reason. We have a "smuggler" friend who is kind enough to send us pictures of Kevin and his family, whenever they are available – usually from Facebook. Linda and I are not allowed access, but one dear friend is. Over the weekend, we received a current picture of Kevin, along with another of Drew and Paisley. This was the first time I had ever seen the face of my granddaughter. She is nearly two years old. It literally took my breath. I had to remind myself to start breathing again. She is beautiful. I could not take my eyes off the picture – both of them standing on a staircase, presumably stairs to the basement of their home. I stared at the picture on my phone for a good five minutes before putting it down. Since then, I have looked at it a hundred times, and even added it as the desktop background on my computer. Nothing could possibly have made me happier than to get that picture. But at the very same time, I was engulfed in the heaviest wave of depression I have ever felt. Two years of her life had passed before I even saw her face. Now nearly seven years had gone by since the one and only time I saw and held Drew. He was just nine days old. It wasn't right. And I was helpless to fix it. How many more years would it be? Would I ever see them in person – spend time with them – get to know them? And what of Kevin – my former best friend who now refuses to acknowledge that I even exist?

Tonight, just a few days after the picture, Morgan called. She does not call often, but when she does, it is always with something good – always happy. You can literally FEEL her love through the phone. She doesn't have to pretend, and never seems inconvenienced at sharing a phone call or spending a little time together. This time, she called to tell me that she had just been asked out on her first date. His name is Soren and she met him in band class at school. A trombone player. They have been spending time together for a couple of months, until, today, he asked her out on a date. Her very first date. I gave her a little grief, of course, about the fact that she is a high school freshman, and he is a senior. I promised her that I was going with them on their date, but only after I had run an FBI background check on the boy. We laughed together for fifteen or twenty minutes as I grilled her with questions about her new discovery. I concluded with a serious admonition that she makes sure that he, or any other boy, treats her like a lady, and that she settles for nothing less, from anyone – ever. I told her how much I love her as we said goodbye.

Morgan will never be able to understand how honored I felt that she would call me with such news as a first date, and a first boyfriend. That single call raised my entire outlook on life a bit. I am sure that it was no big deal to her, but it was a milestone for me that I will never forget. I am truly blessed to have the two greatest grandkids in Morgan and Kalen that a grandpa could wish for. I can only imagine what the other two are like, and how it would feel having them in my life as well.

twenty-five

There are "hawk" days, and there are "buzzard" days...

I love to spend time outdoors. I am truly not a fan of cold weather, but just about any day is better spent outside than in. Summertime, though, requires spending plenty of time at the lake, on the shooting range, even mowing the grass, just enjoying the air and the wide-open spaces, and being anywhere but in the house. I am, likewise, a huge fan of nature – especially, for some reason, birds. I grew up well out in the country, surrounded by woods and pastures, where I could hunt squirrels, rabbits, doves, and even quail now and then – right out my back door – and for a couple of miles in any direction. I live much closer to town, and neighbors, now, but still enjoy watching deer come through the backyard. Squirrels, rabbits, doves, and chipmunks are daily visitors and we have even spotted an occasional fox or coyote. We enjoyed watching a pair of owls as they nested in the pines behind our house last year and raised a couple of babies. It is a pair of red-tailed hawks, however, that keeps me mesmerized. A power line easement along the back border of our property offers a wide-open hunting ground for mice, snakes, rabbits, etc., and the support tower on the corner of our lot offers the perfect lofty rest from which to spot the next meal. These are older hawks, standing nearly 24" tall, with a wingspan well over three feet. These birds are precision hunters and are simply magnificent in flight, or just perched atop the power line tower. But these are only two of the birds that frequently catch my attention.

    I have an uncanny ability to spot a hawk just about anywhere I go. There is rarely a day that passes without my sighting at least one, and often as many as five or six before returning home. I spend a lot of time driving around a large portion of the state on business, as well as frequent trips to the lake. The varied landscape provides multiple encounters with wildlife of all sorts but seldom fails to produce a hawk among the offerings. I don't really concentrate on finding them but often find my eyes drawn to a slight movement or even a distant spec that proves – more often than not – to be a hawk. Linda has often commented that she does not understand how I am able to spot them so easily, as I point them out to her - circling overhead, retrieving prey from the side of the road, or possibly just sitting on a tree branch or power line, well off the roadside. My eyesight is still pretty good, but nothing extraordinary. I happen to believe that there is a far more practical explanation for these "more-often-than-not" sightings – God puts them there. One of the most notable traits of a hawk is its own incredible eyesight. I have often heard (and used) the expression "I am watching you like a hawk". Nothing goes without notice – even the smallest detail. This species of bird is capable of spotting the tiniest morsel of lunch, wiggling through the grass, from heights that present themselves as barely visible from the ground. Then, before the eye can blink or muscle react, this extraordinary being can respond to the slightest flinch from the object of his attention. So, it is with me and God. There is no detail of my life – no matter how small or seemingly unimportant – that escapes His attention. He remains situated high above me with a vantage point that offers a clear view of my every action yet lives close enough to hear even a whisper of a prayer. He "watches" me constantly, standing ready for correction or instruction as I need it. He "watches over" me as well – protecting me from temptations, dangers, and even from my own poor decisions. He constantly looks for opportunities to bless me, even though I never deserve it.

The "hawk" days in my life are those when I position myself closely to God, begin my day with prayer, and listen to, and follow his instructions. It is then that I feel just a little more on top of my day, a little more in charge of the day's events, and just a little more the conqueror than the victim. There comes with this closeness a certain confidence and assurance that allows me to take on the day. That does not mean that everything goes smoothly or exactly the way that I planned. Some of the most hectic days of my life can still be listed in the "hawk" column – just because of the resources at hand that saw me through them. Romans 8:31 says "If God is for us, then who can be against us?". That does not mean that life will not try to bring me down; it just means that it will not – that it cannot succeed.

"Buzzard" days are just the opposite. A buzzard is a far more cowardly bird, attacking and devouring whatever it can find that is already dead, or on its last leg. They are, however, patient, and persistent creatures – perfectly content to circle, and watch, and intimidate their prey, as it grows weaker, and wanders farther and farther from the safety of its protector. On those days when I drift a little outside the warmth of God's protection, I set myself up to fall prey to life's attacks. Tackling the world on my own, and without the assurance He offers, and without His strength to see me through, I am far more likely to just lie down and "die" to the struggles that life will most certainly provide. Problems just seem to pile up, and, before I know it, the day's events have "devoured" me, and life seems a lot less worthwhile. I'm overwhelmed with the weight of the world, and I have totally lost sight of the light and protection of home. I have survived, at best, but offer little value to the world or people around me. The thing is, I get to choose – a hawk day or a buzzard day. I do not get to pick the problems I face – the challenges, the hardships, or the devastations. Those are unavoidable and certain. But I do have access to the help of One who is capable of seeing me through them, with my peace of mind, my sanity, my influence, and my value to those around me, still intact.

twenty-six

Retirement finally came....@ 68 years, 10 months, and 13 days – May 1, 2021. We sold our Fayetteville home of 37 years at the very top of the housing market, for about three times what we had invested 37 years prior. With a house at the lake, it made no sense whatsoever to rent another place, so, with the much-needed help of family, we packed everything into three large storage units, took a modicum of more valuable items with us, and moved to the lake on a full-time basis. About 2 months later, I sold my company to a long-time friend and regular customer and financed it over the next two or three years. No fanfare, no fireworks, no retirement party - no hoopla whatsoever, from anyone - I just stopped working and went home. At least for the most part. I am still helping the new owner get his feet on the ground. But it is now his ground, and his credit card, not mine. No one was surprised, actually. Maybe they all thought it was long past due. I certainly did. Regardless, I am happy for me – a lesson I perfected some time ago. What to do next? So far, I have not even begun to make a dent in the list of projects I would like to get done. I am working on plans for a new house to build for

Linda and I in Arbor Springs Subdivision in Newnan – a somewhat upscale, and definitely out-of-our-league neighborhood. That "top of the housing market" that I mentioned has also pushed building material prices up as much as 450% and pushed product availability out several months in some cases. Obviously, something has to "give" before we can begin construction.

The house we are planning is much too big and much too expensive for what we actually need, but it is just what Linda wants. That, alone, makes it just what I want as well. At least, I think, our money will be well protected there. I was caught completely off guard when Linda expressed, through a smattering of tears, that she would finally be able to enjoy the two things she had always wanted in a home – a brick foundation, and a neighborhood with other people. Who knew? Who would have ever guessed that those two things, both so simple and easy to achieve, would top the wish list. If only I had known 20 years ago. It makes good sense though. Since she left her job at New Hope, she has really been at a loss without the people around her that made up her second family. There is a void there that nothing else can fill. Maybe now she can begin to rebuild friendships around her with a new group of candidates.

The original plan, after the sale of our house, was to sell the lake house as well, and build one home, somewhere on the lake. After months of searching, we located a PERFECT lot, the PERFECT size, on a PERFECT part of the lake, in a PERFECT subdivision – with three hundred feet of waterfront no less! The goal was to get the large home that Linda wanted, to build where our money was best protected long term, and to get down to just one house to maintain (my own primary goal). I had the purchase contract for the property in my hand, along with a pen to sign it, when Linda and I began to talk about "life at the lake", and what it would be like to live there for more than just a weekend at the time. After an hour or so of pros and cons, it finally came out – she could not see herself adjusting to the isolation (privacy for some of us) that this location would offer. There were numerous houses around us, but, admittedly, nearly every single one was a "weekend" home leaving almost no one around for most of the week. It was a pretty good drive, as well, to get out of the subdivision and drive to surrounding shopping, restaurants, etc. It was also a long drive to see the kids, and back to all things familiar. The lake itself was certainly convenient, but little else was. Instead of signing the offer, I filed it away in the trash can under my desk and called a disappointed realtor the next morning to break the news. It was absolutely the right thing to do… but the hardest part of this entire transition for me. I look forward to building again. Design and construction are, after all, my passion in life. At the same time, I do love life at the lake – smaller, simpler, slower, less complicated, not to mention less expensive. I can tell, already, that I am going to miss it.

    Life at the lake takes a little adjustment. The wheels turn here at a much slower rate. One thing I have learned from dealing with people here for a number of years, is that no native of Alabama is going to be rushed – not because of your schedule or deadline, not from any panic you might exhibit, not even for money. The length of the work week is determined by how long it takes to earn enough money to pay this week's bills, with a little beer money left over. Any longer than that is a waste of energy, and cuts into fishing and hunting time. There is a sacred pace that simply must not be violated. What is more, it's contagious. I occasionally find myself stuck behind a slow car without any opportunity to pass for miles, but instead of frantically searching for any opportunity to get around or praying that the car ahead will turn at the next corner, I have become content to simply trail behind, at my captor's crawl, and even enjoy it. Weird, and unfamiliar, but a welcome change in pace.

    There is a fairly long, winding road that leads to our house after you leave "civilization" behind. It is dotted along the way with an occasional, modest, older home, most adorned with old, lazy dogs and more, rusty, junkyard-worthy cars, than seem necessary for any yard. The question that so often crosses my mind is "How in the world do these people make a living?" There are a few signs of farming and a few pastures with a handful of cattle, but no retail businesses, no factories, not even a gas station nearby that might offer employment. But the people here are determined, to say the least. Some, I am sure, make the long trek into town each day, to work in shopping centers, hospitals, schools, and factories there. The majority, however, manage to squeeze a living out of what they know how to do, with their own hands, by themselves, and most with more than just one skill on display. Small business thrives here. Now I would never want to have it thought that I make fun of the truly imaginative people around our area – I am absolutely impressed with what they are able to accomplish. But I must admit, I am somewhat entertained by the unusual combinations of businesses that litter the countryside. As an example, one "his and hers ' home business just down the street from us pairs a husband as a realtor and a wife as a hairstylist. A good pair, each with their own specialty. Nearly everyone here, it seems, sells barbeque, fish bait, or both. Two blocks away is actually a combination restaurant/art gallery/bait shop – one-stop shopping. Just one step off the more recognizable normal is the local HVAC contractor who also does plumbing work (quite a common pairing) but who also sells fireworks (not quite as common). But there is yet another level. We have a tree service that also repairs transmissions. A nearby gutter contractor does brush mulching as well. Just to the South is an income tax preparation/welding service, or at least until recently. The welding side of the business closed and was replaced with, of course, a towing service. There is even a garage door company that sells (naturally) rabbits. Yep, live rabbits. I must hand it to all of them – they love what they do and do what they love – whatever that happens to be – and even manage to earn a little money at it. How could anyone find fault with that? Yes, I am going to miss living at the lake, for sure.

twenty-seven

The year is 2020 and it has been littered with new terminology and catchphrases. Quarantine is an all-too-familiar routine. We have come to hear, as quite commonplace, things like "social distancing", "contact tracing", "new normal", "virtual learning", and "stay-at-home stocks" – all courtesy of Covid-19 – the Coronavirus. Not just a neighborhood thing, but a full-blown, worldwide, pandemic, with no prevention, no treatment, and no cure. Elbow bumps have taken the place of the ever-familiar handshake. Face masks are the fashion must-have of the day. Restaurants serve via pick-up or delivery only – dining in is rare. Those restaurants that could not adapt to some sort of drive-thru format closed – temporarily at first, then later, many, for good. Churches closed along with the eating establishments, as did bars, theaters, schools, retail shops, malls, banks, and sporting events – from little league to major league – recreational to professional. Even government offices appear dark. Foreign travel - suspended. Hundreds of flights have been canceled. Cruise ships, worldwide, sit, empty, tied to the dock. Even the trading floor of the New York Stock Exchange was off-limits for several days.

With 2021 coming to an end, the entire world is now nearing 2 years into a Covid 19 pandemic. Serious stuff, though you would never know it looking at how people shop, attend church, sporting events, and concerts. Linda and I are now three vaccines into the process, and, so far, have managed to avoid the plague entirely. Yet, half of the nation still refuses to get shots. The reasons range anywhere from blaming religion, to practicing holistic medicine, all the way to conspiracy theories that the government is attempting to infect us with some DNA-altering drugs in order to establish some kind of mind control! The world has simply gone collectively mad. At first, the entire situation was only a matter of statistics – something that happened to someone else, in some other state. Businesses were closed, schools shut down, no church, no travel… not much of anything. Rather rapidly, reality flooded closer to home, as neighbors began reporting that they knew people who had contracted Covid-19, some even hospitalized. Then can the reports of hospitalizations in our county, then the death toll in the county. When restrictions began to lift, our church began services again, right away, and much too early.

On Monday morning following the first service, an email went out stating that someone who had attended the service on the previous day had been diagnosed with Covid-19. Several other members came down with it over the next few weeks, and, finally, one actually died. That first death was only the beginning, however, of the toll that the disease would take in our church, and the entire community – and even our own family. Todd's mom, Nancy, and dad, Ed, both came down with Covid-19. They fought it as long as they could, but neither was improving, with Nancy suffering the most from the ailment. Ed dropped off his wife at the hospital for a checkup and treatment and returned home (absolutely no visitors were allowed in the hospital), never suspecting that it would be the last time he would see her alive. Nancy lasted less than a week, while Ed gradually began to improve – only to face the rest of his life on his own.

As the year progressed, schools became virtual – Wendy and Todd were teaching from home. Teaching MUSIC from home, mind you – middle school BAND to be exact. A totally impossible task. More people worked from home, in every profession, than the number who went to an actual office. High school and college graduations were canceled from coast to coast – including Morgans. This was her senior high school year – no band banquets, no prom, no senior trips, no graduation, - nothing. Schedules and routines as we had known them had ALL changed, with no end in sight. Now Christmas was approaching, and family gatherings were discouraged, especially with family members who had to travel any distance. Our larger family, at the last minute, decided to cancel as well, for fear of the disease and the likelihood of spreading it. With Wendy, Todd, and both kids still healthy – and Linda and I as well – we decided to maintain our tradition of getting together as an immediate family at Wendy and Todd's house and celebrate Christmas with them and our grandchildren. Just a week before Christmas, Wendy and Todd began to feel ill, made an appointment for testing, and were both diagnosed with, what would turn out to be, a month-long bout with Covid. We managed to get together for a little while after Christmas to exchange our gifts, but it hardly seemed the same. The tradition had been missed, and Christmas Day was spent very quietly and uneventfully for all of us.

Today is exactly one year later – Christmas Day again. With Linda and I at the lake house, and too far away for the family to travel to us (not to mention too little space to entertain everyone), the family gathering was slated for Linda's brother's house. Mike and Vaughn graciously agreed to host, and plans were all in the works. A few weeks before, Mike and Vaughn took a Florida vacation with friends. Both of their friends were feeling poorly for the entire trip. After returning home, first Vaughn, then Mike also began feeling ill, as well, finally visiting a doctor, and were both diagnosed with a sinus infection. Thankfully, all tested negative for COVID-19, but the risk of infecting the rest of the family, once again, prompted the cancellation of our annual family gathering.

Plans were still on for our visit to spend Christmas with the kids. This year, in fact, we were going up on Christmas Eve, intending to spend a couple of days with them. Linda and I opened our modest gifts to one another on the evening of the 23rd and awoke on the morning of the 24th to begin packing the car. More clothes than we probably needed, certainly more desserts than any of us needed, and gifts all around, of course, packed the entire cargo area of her SUV. Linda was in the car, and I was locking the door to the house when the phone rang. It seems Kalen had been spending a lot of time with friends for the past several days who, one by one, had been diagnosed with COVID-19. Kalen was feeling fine, but, just as a precaution, Morgan had left to find a COVID-19 DIY test to make sure he did not have it as well. He had gotten his third vaccination just a week ago and was showing no symptoms - yet. "Give us 30 minutes before you leave", she said, to get the test results.

He tested positive. There was nothing left to do but unload the car and settle in for a second year without Christmas. More importantly, without family. Maybe it is because I have gotten older, or maybe it comes from not being able to get together any time that we want, but FAMILY has become, more than ever, such a vital part of my life. I miss them all. I need them all. I can tell that Linda feels the same way. Simply nothing is more important. Linda made us a wonderful lunch – over the top – and we settled into an afternoon of Christmas movies on the Hallmark Channel while Sabrina snoozed on the couch beside us. Maybe just to add to my own despair, I sent Kevin a text, wishing him and his family a Merry Christmas. There was no response, again, just as I figured. I had written to him a couple of weeks ago, trying to make him understand how important he is to me, how much I miss him, and how much I still love him. There was no response to the letter either. No surprise – just more disappointment. Maybe Covid will be over soon. Maybe Kevin will call……

More bad news was to follow just a few months later….

I buried the best friend I ever had today, under the streetlight, near the edge of the lake, in the pouring rain. The rain seemed only fitting, given how much I miss her. Sabrina was 13 years old – a 2 ½ pound Yorkie/Chihuahua mix. Full grown, and just about the size of a small squirrel, she could hardly see over a Coke can placed in front of her. Linda and I found her from a breeder in North Georgia when she was just five weeks old. We actually had to wait two more weeks for her to be old enough to leave her mom, and big enough to get her first shots, before we could take her home. Her parents were about 6 ½ or 7 pounds each, and we fully expected Sabrina to be about the same size, but she never even made it to half that. At seven weeks, she was small enough to stand with all four feet on the toe of my size 8 shoe, with room to spare. We worried that we might step on her at first, but soon realized just how quick and agile she was, and well adept at staying out of harm's way. We got used to one another very quickly and managed to avoid any injuries…for any of us…throughout her life.

It is amazing just how attached you can become to such a tiny little intrusion into your life, never intending to, to begin with. Though we tried to do everything in our power to make her life as full, and healthy, and happy as we possibly could, it was her who brought joy into our lives in much greater proportion. She had become family. I think maybe one of the reasons she meant so much to me might be that she arrived in our lives just about the same time that Kevin left us. Don't misunderstand – she could never replace the loss of my son by any means, but she did help to fill one small corner of the huge hole that was left when he moved away. I still miss them both, every day, and imagine that I always will.

twenty-eight

I was driving this morning, with the radio playing, skipping through the mindless dribble offered as entertainment by the morning show host. In an effort to stir up some sort of controversial banter, he offered the question to his audience, "Do you believe in ghosts?", and asked listeners to call in with accounts of "supernatural" things that had happened to them that had no reasonable explanation (as though people were actually interested in anything he was saying). He had no takers, and his segment failed miserably. He floundered with the subject for half an hour or so, then gave up on the segment entirely. But it did serve to bring a memory or two back to my own mind. Now, while I am not a believer in the stereotypical, white-sheet-wearing, Casper-type ghost, I certainly do believe that there are forces – spirits, if you will – that exist around us, that we are sometimes allowed to witness, or, at other times, allowed to interact with. I recall several such incidents that I still have no explanation for, and I am convinced that they came from somewhere other than God. Some may be explained scientifically. Others, not so much. The occurrences were years apart from one another, and each one was a totally different experience, however, oddly, each one occurred within a few yards of the same spot: in the worship center of New Hope Baptist Church. Believe, if you will, or not – your choice.

The first one came in the middle of a Spring afternoon, and with a witness. I was meeting with an electrician and former church member, Mike, to discuss some electrical and lighting changes that we wanted to make to the balcony lighting system. We walked the areas in question, then drifted down to the front row of the balcony, near the center of the auditorium, and sat down to discuss our options and the costs involved. The auditorium lights were off, but with the weather outside bright and sunny, there was plenty of light streaming through the lower-level front windows to make movement around the balcony quite easy.

We sat facing forward, with a clear view of the full balcony curve, the seating on the floor below, the full width of the stage, and the back wall of the stage that stretches from the stage floor to the wood-beamed ceiling, nearly 40' above. As we sat and talked, we were both distracted by a sudden, and very bright, flash of light, just to the right of center of the stage. Mike gasped and asked, "Did I just see what I think I saw?". I responded at the exact same instance that he answered his own question, and we both exclaimed – "LIGHTNING!". "I thought so", he said. We sat for a moment, still dumbfounded at what had happened. Not quite a full minute passed, with us both still staring at the stage, and it happened again. A second bolt of lightning originated within the building, just below the ceiling peak, and traveled to the stage floor, striking just about ten feet to the right of the first. Our surprise now turned to concern at the possible damage that might have been caused, or the danger involved in the lightning strikes. What if it had happened while the building was occupied? Could it ever happen again? And suddenly it did! A third strike hit the floor, another fifteen' to the right of the second. Remember, the weather outside was perfectly clear. No rain, no storms, no wind – just clear blue skies and white puffy clouds above. Mike and I waited for quite some time before walking down to the stage to check for fire or other damage. We found no damage, and no evidence whatsoever of the strikes. I have not seen it happen since or been told of anyone else who has.

The next time I had no witness, and this one was not so much an event, exactly, as a feeling. I am not sure I can even accurately describe what happened without seeming overly dramatic, but here is the account, as accurately as I can describe it. I was working very late in the audio/video room, just off the hallway that runs behind the stage in the main auditorium. Late nights were not so unusual, since I had the responsibility of a lot of the audio and video editing that our church produced. This particular night I was working on producing the hour-long sermon tape that would be aired on the radio the following Sunday morning. It was nearing midnight. There was no one else in the building, or on the entire church property, for that matter. The only sound was literally that of my own breath and my movement about the room.

Though completely focused on my task at hand, I suddenly was distracted by the unmistakable feeling that something was watching me. Notice that I said something, not someone. Don't ask how I knew the difference. Many times, I have felt the presence of another person in the room with me, before I ever saw or heard them, then turned to find someone actually standing there. There is something about the acoustics, or the temperature, or just the volume of air in the room that changes. This was not the same.

Whatever this was, was something dark and formidable; something threatening, viscous, and eminent. Something huge. Though the mid-August night was hot and stuffy, I felt a cold chill come over me, causing me to shiver from head to toe. With it came a gripping fear, unlike anything I had ever felt. Even now, as I am recounting the event, the chill has returned. I quickly glanced around at the empty room, recalling that the only door into the room was locked, in an attempt to reassure myself that my late-night imagination was all that was a play there. I am not the type who is afraid of the dark and have spent many late nights working in this very room – all quite comfortably. The sight of the empty room around me was no comfort this time. The feeling grew stronger. The thought actually crossed my mind that I might not ever make it out of the building. There was no time to waste.

After several minutes of being unable to escape the feeling, I dropped what I had in my hand onto the soundboard in front of me and bolted for the door. With all the lights and equipment still on, I slammed the door behind me and literally ran down the hall toward the back door. I shoved the steel door open and lunged for the door handle on my truck, parked just outside the rear hallway exit. As I jumped into the driver's seat and started the truck, I locked the doors and sped out of the parking lot and off the property. Looking back, I do not recall locking the door to the church or setting the alarm. I drove the short half-mile home as quickly as my vehicle would take me, but I had not left the fear, nor the chill behind. It was still with me. Now in the driveway, I threw open the truck door, and again, literally ran toward the front door of my home. Inside, I closed the door behind me, locked it, and set the house alarm. It was only now that the chill began to pass, and the fear slowly drained from my soul. It took several minutes to clear my mind and regain composure. There would be other late (even later) nights to come spent working at the church, but never another night alone in that room.

    Several years later came one of those times when the fear came only after everything was over – the fear of what might have been. I had been running the sound mixer for a rehearsal of the annual church Christmas presentation. This was a "technical" rehearsal where we had focused on adjusting every microphone, every speaker, correcting the tone, the volume – every aspect of sound that was controlled by the 64-channel Yamaha mixing board in front of me – and that was a lot. Altogether, there were between 550 and 600 buttons, knobs, and sliders on the face of that nearly 6' wide mammoth piece of electronics. We had just spent several hours making sure every one of them was exactly at their peak performance.

    Rehearsal ended, and it was nearing 10:30 p.m. I put a cover over the board, powered down all of the equipment in the balcony sound booth, and descended the stairs to the main floor below. Our music director, John, exited the building just ahead of me, leaving me the last person to leave the sanctuary. I set the building alarm system and locked the door behind me. The maintenance staff has long since been gone and the property was deserted. The next day was to be a full day of dress rehearsal. It was Saturday morning, and the maintenance staff was off for the early part of the day, so I returned ahead of everyone else to open up the building and begin setting up for the day's rehearsal.

I walked up to the still-dark sound booth, and, in reverse order from the previous night, flipped on the lights, powered up all the equipment, and removed the cover from the soundboard. Something was off, but, at first, it was not clear just what it was. Then it hit me – every single control on the soundboard had been changed. Not one knob, button, or slider was in the position I had left it the night before. John arrived shortly afterward, and I can still recall him standing in front of the board without saying a word, in total disbelief. The alarm had not been disturbed all night. It seemed that the board had been changed by someone who did not need a key to get in, and someone with no respect for our efforts on the previous day.

The most recent incident was possibly the most dramatic of all, and with a witness as well (sort of). Strangely, there was no fear at all this time. It was just after 1:30 a.m. (yep, another one of those late nights) on the main floor of the sanctuary. I had been working, alone, on creating sets and props for yet another Christmas program, out in the lobby. Needing something in the sanctuary, I turned on all of the house lights from a switch at the back entrance door and walked down the center aisle to the front of the stage. As I approached the stage, even knowing that I was the only person in the building, I began to hear voices coming from behind me. I turned to see who was there and realized that I was hearing the voice of a little girl and it was coming from the balcony. The balcony was fully lit, so I turned my attention there, near the top, on the far-right side of the balcony from the stage, where the sound seemed to originate. There was no one there, but the faint, tiny voice continued, then was followed by the voice of a young boy. Still, no one was in sight. The voices were obvious, but not clear enough to make out the conversation. They were the happy voices of the two young children, mixed with laughter. They were getting closer. They were soon joined by a conversation between an older man and woman, Mom and Dad maybe, as they all drew closer and began to pass to the right, across the balcony. The four of them continued to laugh and talk as they crossed the balcony. The voices continued to weaken, and eventually fade out, still with no sign of a person actually being there. This time I felt no fear whatsoever. The family seemed friendly enough and I did not feel any threat from them – even though I couldn't even see them. A strange feeling indeed.

The oddest part of this episode came almost exactly one year later. There was a substantial group of us, once again in the sanctuary, in the process of constructing the 40' Christmas tree centerpiece for this year's performance. I was taking a break on the front row pew, along with a couple of friends, including one member of the maintenance staff. I am not sure how the conversation began, but one of my coworkers was asking about working in the building late at night. I began to share my "balcony family" experience with him, but before I could get into any details, the maintenance member interrupted me. As a newer member of the team, it often fell to him to catch the later shift at the church, so he had spent a number of late nights in the church himself. "Wait," he said, "are you talking about the family who walks through the balcony late at night?" As he said it, he pointed to the exact point where I had heard the voices originate and drew his finger across the balcony in the direction that I had heard them travel. He had encountered the late-night residents as well and acknowledged that he had heard them on more than one occasion.

It may be true that I have lost my mind, and imagined it all, if that is what you choose to believe. But at least I have company.

twenty-nine

Perhaps this book-writing thing would go a little smoother if I started with an outline. I hated doing those things in school . . . such a waste of time. "A good outline forms the skeleton that supports the body of the work." Yeah, right. But what have I got to lose? Nothing else has worked.

Let's see what we have . . .

Outline

It is perfectly alright to meddle in other people's business, if you know what you are doing.
Nope, that won't work. Try again.

Sometimes it's alright to meddle in other . . .
Still not it. One more time – different approach.

I am who I am because of them.
    a.   The challenge of my own child.
    b.   God picks up the slack.

That's better; what else?

A son doubles the challenge.

God told me.
    a.   Sometimes we hear Him.
    b.   Sometimes His voice is drowned out.
    c.   Sometimes He just doesn't get the credit.

Yeah, I even got that "a, b, c," thing working . . . or was the "1, 2, 3," supposed to come first. No matter, just go on. I'm drifting again.

Revenge on a bush.

Recliners and Sunday naps are overrated, anyway.

Good one! There could be a couple of chapters on that.

Life in the Navy.

Surviving the insanity.

Alligators are not your friends.

Junior electrician.

Dreams that can be shared are rare.

Dream anyway.

Poem to Wendy.

Unlikely friends

Life with my grandfather.

An unselfish prayer.

Christmas is a reality check.

Grass is gonna' grow – learn to adapt.

Not even a heart attack…..

Mom & Dad's turn to enjoy a little.

Loss greater than death.

God is in control.
Hallelujah!

Losing Mom & Dad.

PSA tests are no fun at all.

Instructions to Wendy.

Reading glasses and AARP ads.

Old man's rant.

Hawk days and buzzard days.

Retirement….at last!

Who stole Christmas?

I don't believe in ghosts.

Oh, what's the use? Who in this world would ever be interested in anything I might write, even if I was any good at it? And I'm not! What made me ever think I could do this? The poem wasn't half bad. Maybe poetry . . . no, just kidding myself again. I know – I could write a song – country, maybe. That should be easy. I wonder if Wal-Mart has some of that paper with the lines . . .

Postlude

I'm sure I never said it then, but, wherever you are, thank you, Mrs. Stokes, as well as so many others, for being a little meddlesome – for caring enough to point (or shove) me in the right direction when I needed it, whether I wanted it or not.

I'm sure I don't say it <u>often enough</u>, but thank you, God, for always picking up right where I run out of answers and carrying me to places that I could never have dreamed of; for watching me, for protecting me, and for blessing me beyond belief.

Thank you, Mom and Dad, for actively, and deliberately, teaching me the difference between right and wrong, the rewards of the former, along with the consequences of the latter, and always pointing me toward the Lord Jesus Christ as my anchor and deliverer.

Despite all my efforts to give to my children, I remain indebted to them – for teaching me some of the most basic, and most cherished, lessons in life, while effortlessly multiplying the quality of my own life exponentially.

Even given an extra lifetime to do so, I would never be able to tell my wife, Linda, what a foundation she provides for my life, how she fills my days, and my thoughts. The mere concept of love alone does not begin to describe how I feel about her. She is why I continue to breathe.

One final update . . .

Andrew Kevin Entrekin, my grandson, was born on December 18, 2009. I held him only once and saw him last when he was nine days old. Regrettably, I have not seen him since, nor spoken to my son – his choosing, not mine – and I still have no idea as to why. My granddaughter was born on January 15, 2015. I just recently learned that her name is Paisley, but still have not seen her or know that I ever will. Chip came along on February 27, 2018. I have no idea what his full name is, or if he will ever be told that I even exist. My love for Kevin continues and remains as strong as ever . . . always will. I wish nothing more than to see him again, as well as Drew, Paisley, and Chip, and to make them a part of my life once again. I am finding it harder each day to function without them but will never give up hope of their return

Just recently, years after Wendy's questions about my forgiveness ability, I have begun polite, simple conversations with Rob whenever we find ourselves together. I cannot truly say I have totally forgiven him, but I have come to realize that life is too short to spend it making myself miserable over the past, and past mistakes. I truly want to forgive him. I miss the time we used to spend together, and hope, somehow, to restore that friendship. Perhaps, it is me who needs forgiveness, as well. Still, my soul remains fearful for his future – his business, his current marriage, and his health.

Morgan and Kalen are the true lights of my life. I grow prouder every day of who they are becoming. I love nothing more than spending time with them and consider it a rare honor to be called "grandpa" by two such talented and loving individuals.

My love for Wendy grows ever stronger by the day. I admire, now more than ever, her courage and her strength, and her reliance on God. I am grateful that she allows me to be a part of her life and I truly hope that time will help to totally heal her and her children. I am grateful, too, that she chooses to share her two wonderful children with me. I could only hope to achieve her level of fortitude and integrity. She remains my hero.

Todd is an absolute Godsend. I have never seen such an anchor in a storm nor a more perfect fit for Wendy, Morgan, and Kalen, as well as our entire family. Thank you, Lord, for your perfect timing, and for another son, that I have truly grown to love, as well as respect.

I pray for all of them regularly.

www.ingramcontent.com/pod-product-compliance
Lightning Source LLC
Chambersburg PA
CBHW070104080526
44586CB00013B/1181